THE SCENOGRAPHY OF JOSEF SVOBODA

Josef Svoboda in front of a photograph of his production of Prokofiev's *The Engagement in the Cloister* (1947).

THE SCENOGRAPHY

OF

JOSEF SVOBODA

By JARKA BURIAN

WESLEYAN UNIVERSITY PRESS

Middletown, Connecticut

ISBN: 0-8195-6032-4

Library of Congress catalog card number: 77-153101

Manufactured in the United States of America

First paperback edition, 1974; second printing, 1977

CONTENTS

LIST OF ILLUSTRATIONS

Most of the uncredited photographs were made by Josef Svoboda.

PREFACE

Most of the material for this book was gathered at first hand in Prague, where I lived for ten months between September 1968 and August 1969 on a research grant cosponsored by the American Inter-University Committee on Travel Grants and the Czechoslovakian Ministry of Education. During that time I had the privilege of extended personal acquaintance with Josef Svoboda and his work and of access to numerous sources of information relating to his theatre world. Professor Svoboda's studio and his archives were made available to me, and I was able to follow his work from drawing board to model to production on more than one occasion. I especially valued the hours that we spent in conversations focussed on but not limited to his productions and the principles that they embodied. I tape-recorded about a dozen of these informal sessions and have drawn on them in many sections of this book. Since my departure from Prague, I have communicated with Svoboda by letter and by tape-recording. Consequently, I have been able to refer to significant examples of his work following the 1968–69 season. Moreover, I was able to visit with Svoboda again briefly in Prague in the fall of 1970, at which time I was brought up to date on his most recent productions, a representative number of which I have described in Appendix B.

Many people and organizations were generous with their assistance and suggestions, which I acknowledge with gratitude. The State University of New York at Albany encouraged my applying for the research grant and granted me a leave of absence when I received the grant. Clinton J. Atkinson was instrumental in initiating the Svoboda project and provided encouragement throughout. Howard Miller read the manuscript in its later stages and offered many helpful suggestions. Impossible as it is to cite all of the countless instances of scholarly and personal aid that I received in Czechoslovakia, I do wish to mention at least a few of the people most directly concerned with this project: Dr. Eva Soukupová, Director of the Theatre Institute in Prague, and her expert staff of coworkers in research, documentation, and publications dealing with the Czechoslovakian theatre; Ing. Miroslav Kouřil and the resources of the Scenographic Institute; the immediate coworkers of Josef Svoboda in the scenic workshops and studios of the National Theatre, especially Svoboda's secretary, Jaroslav Schneider, and Svoboda's optical and lighting expert, Ing. Miroslav Pflug.

A special note of appreciation and thanks is due Dr. Jaromír Svoboda, the official photographer of the National Theatre, for his gracious permission to let me use his superb photographs in documenting the major part of this study.

Above all, I thank my wife Grayce for her practical assistance, productive criticism, and comfort throughout the entire period of my work on this study.

*A note on documentation and translation: quotations from the tape-recorded interviews with Svoboda are indicated by an asterisk (*). Among Svoboda's filed material and personal scrapbooks, considerable material appears in the form of clippings that provide little or no indication of author, title, date, or other identification; I have indicated such documentation as was available. All translations are mine. I have followed a pattern of translating Czech titles the first time they appear in this book and thereafter using English titles except in documentary material.

INTRODUCTION

As he passed his fiftieth birthday, in 1970, Josef Svoboda was in mid-career and at the height of his powers as an architecturally trained stage designer or, as he prefers to be called, scenographer. His work has been applauded in most theatre centers of the Western world, and he is without a doubt the most prolific, vital, and sought-after designer in Europe today. The sheer quantity of his productivity is in itself remarkable: in twenty-five years he has designed nearly four hundred productions, roughly split between the operatic and dramatic repertoires, for most of the major theatres of Europe.

During much of this period Svoboda has been chief designer and technical director of the National Theatre in Prague, a repertory complex that consists of three ensembles (drama, opera, ballet) and performs in three theatres. Each season from September to July it presents sixty to seventy different productions, of which approximately fifteen are new, the rest being held over from previous seasons.[1] Although he designs less than half of the productions and has a large and capable staff of more than three hundred, Svoboda has been ultimately responsible for all technical and scenic elements in the three theatres.

He has, moreover, taught at various times, and he is currently Professor of Architecture at the School of Fine and Applied Arts in Prague. Still another area of his creativity is evident in his exhibition work at major international expositions. At Brussels, in 1958, for example, he won three gold medals for his work displayed in the Czechoslovak pavilion, and his several kinetic and film projects were among the most popular attractions at Expo 67, Montreal.

Svoboda's name is chiefly associated with a full-scale artistic exploitation of the latest mechanical, electronic, and optical devices, many of which he and his staff have developed themselves, with the so-called kinetic stage, with wide-ranging use of sophisticated lighting and projection techniques,

1. A brief indication of the context provided by contemporary Czechoslovakian theatre may be useful: there are over sixty professional theatres in Czechoslovakia, comprising over one-hundred professional ensembles. All theatres are non-profit and state-supported at an average of two-thirds of their expenses. All theatres, moreover, consist of permanent companies and perform in repertory, which means that several productions alternate in a given span of time instead of one production being performed consecutively. The average theatre presents approximately twelve different productions each season, of which almost half are new. The repertoire is international, with approximately half of the productions being native works.

and with radical assaults on the limitations of the still dominant proscenium theatre. In this and other respects his work recalls the ideal of the artists of the Bauhaus school of the 1920s: "a new synthesis of art and technology."[2] His work has also been related to that of such giants of modern stage theory and practise as Appia, Craig, and Piscator, as well as the Soviet avant-garde of the twenties. All such associations, however, while useful in suggesting the significance and scope of Svoboda's efforts, still require considerable qualification to define the essential features of his talent.

He is, for example, less a theoretical visionary than were either Appia or Craig, but he surpasses them in his mastery of sophisticated materials and techniques as well as in sheer practical experience. Many of his productions recall the emphasis on scenic dynamics and the stage-as-mechanism evident in the early post-revolutionary work of the Soviet theatricalists Meyerhold and Tairov, but Svoboda's greater technical sophistication and less tendentious approach provide a generally subtler, more emotive experience.[3] Similarly, although some of his most audacious work in the fusion of film and stage relates to the earlier work of Piscator, Svoboda has attained a more complex level of creation with a new, hybrid form combining actor and screened image.

In brief, his work represents a synthesis, a refinement, and a masterful application of the theories and practical experiments that are considered the coordinates of modern stage design and production. More than anyone else in contemporary scenography (one is tempted to say, *uniquely*), he embodies a union of artist, scientist, and professional theatre worker. Technically a master of his complex medium, thoroughly conversant with the realities of theatrical production—the pressures of deadlines, budgets, personnel supervision, and inter-artistic cooperation—he is essentially a superb theatre artist applying his creative imagination to the scenic fundamentals of space, light, and movement.

To a marked degree his career has been built on a series of inner, dialectical tensions: the new and the old, the radical and the conservative, technical bravura and poetic humanism. And supplementing his basic synthesizing method is an inherent pragmatism: he is not committed to any single production mode or design theory. Although a striking innovator, he has genuine respect for traditional forms and simple, limited means when they suit the occasion. Master of the proscenium theatre, he is nonetheless plagued by its limitations, which he constantly strives to overcome in order to break through

2. Walter Gropius, introduction to *The Theatre of the Bauhaus* (Middletown, Conn., 1961), p. 7.

3. "Svoboda's work in Novosibirsk and Moscow, and the exhibit of his work in 1961 [in Moscow] reminded the Soviet theatre of its own traditions, Eisenstein's montages, the heritage of the constructivists and the artists of the Kamerny theatre of the twenties and thirties." L. P. Solnceva, "Der Regisseur und der Bühnenbildner," *Interscena* 68 (Winter 1967), 5:52.

Svoboda in his studio-office. Suspended slightly to the left of his head is the model for his production of *The Anabaptists*.

Svoboda at his drawing board, as reflected in a prototype version of a pneumatic mirror that he now uses in his scenography.

to new forms which may, ironically, wipe out the basis for many of his most impressive techniques.

Precisely because even his seemingly extravagant scenic displays are anchored by a respect for basic craftsmanship and scientific discipline, and because of his pragmatism, his multiform experimentation, his urge toward creativity based on synthesis rather than exclusiveness, and above all his rejection of the narrow connotations of stage "design" in favor of the more inclusive demands of "scenography," he may well prove to be this era's actualization of Craig's ideal, the "artist of the theatre," as well as the artist-scientist to realize Piscator's and Brecht's hopes for "a theatre that would truly belong to our century."[4]

At mid-career, Svoboda is clearly still evolving and in no way settled into a neatly definable or predictable pattern, yet the development of his career is traceable, his artistic principles and methods may be examined, and his most representative work may be illustrated and annotated. That is the intention of this book.

4. Erwin Piscator, "The Theatre Can Belong to Our Century," in *The Theory of the Modern Stage,* ed. Eric Bentley (Baltimore, 1968), p. 473.

PART I. LIFE AND PRINCIPLES

For the sake of convenience, Josef Svoboda's career may be considered in five periods, the last of which is still in progress. The multiplicity of his interests and talents is evident even in the earliest period, which leads up to his twenty-fifth year.

Josef Svoboda was born of Czech parents on May 10, 1920, in Čáslav, a small but prosperous city lying some fifty miles east of Prague, in the agricultural area of central Bohemia. His father was a cabinet-maker by profession, but economic conditions forced him to expand his work to general carpentry and furniture manufacture in the late 1920s.

Josef, an only child, attended the local liberal-arts, Latin-based gymnasium, and he was accepted for entrance to the Philosophic Faculty of Prague's Charles University in 1939. In the meantime, however, his energies had already been channeled in two significant directions: he had spent two of his adolescent years mastering the craft of carpentry and furniture manufacture in his father's small factory, and, as early as his fifteenth year, he had begun to display marked talent in painting and theatre design, as became evident in two subsequent exhibitions of his work in 1940 and in 1941. The exhibitions consisted of oils, chiefly still-life paintings and exteriors, and stage designs and sketches. A brief newspaper account of the second exhibition contained a prophetic observation: "scenic work undoubtedly gives Svoboda the greatest opportunity to assert his rich plastic and spatial imagination."[1]

Before that, however, the fateful year of 1939 had marked the first of several decisive turning points in Svoboda's career. His schooling and interests were already versatile, but despite his acquired craftsmanship in carpentry it was clear that he intended to pursue work in the fine arts and classical university studies. In the fall of 1939, however, the German occupants of Bohemia, reacting to student protests against the occupation, closed down the universities. World War II had begun, and Svoboda's academic career was, at best, deferred. After family consultation it was decided that he should pursue a practical education, building upon his early, unofficial training in his father's factory, and thereby also avoiding forced draft into the German labor camps. He entered an advanced vocational school for master carpentry in Prague and completed a two-year course with distinction in 1941; several of his designs were published in a trade journal during his second year of study. Subse-

1. An untitled, anonymous newspaper clipping (December 1941).

quently, he completed an additional two years of study (1941–43) in a special industrial-technical school in Prague devoted to interior architecture. During these years he designed and built many of the pieces of furniture and cabinetry that are still used in his home in Prague today. His four years of formal study qualified him as a skilled craftsman as well as a candidate for professional architectural training.

During the same period, his extra-curricular interest in painting continued and, more important, his active participation in theatre increased. He began to work with a group of amateurs in Čáslav, and once again we find references to him in local newspaper reviews, which suggest future directions. Commenting on a production of a minor Czech play in February 1942, an anonymous critic wrote, "The use of modern technical elements in scenic design by the young Čáslav designer Josef Svoboda allowed the values of the play, characters, and actors to emerge."[2] A subsequent Čáslav production, in May 1942, elicited a review that noted Svoboda's combining scenery with slide projections and went on to add that "Svoboda's contribution gave the play a poetic form . . . it was the most serious artistic element of the production."[3]

After the temporary completion of his technical studies in 1943, Svoboda taught part-time in secondary vocational and craft schools, but was also able to devote more time and attention to theatre. Supplementing his inherent interest in the stage was his acquaintance with intensely dedicated young theatre artists and writers in Prague. With Svoboda as their main organizer, they formed a semi-professional ensemble known as the New Group and in the fall of 1943 acquired makeshift theatre quarters in Prague's Smetana Museum. Theatre activity in occupied Bohemia was an intermittent affair, heavily censored and short in personnel. Nevertheless, although the significant prewar avant-garde, led by such men as Burian, Honzl, and Frejka, had been disbanded, their influence persisted, if only in temporarily assembled and shoestring ensembles like the New Group. The ensemble staged two productions in the Smetana Museum in 1943: a dramatization of Hölderlin's *Empedokles* in October, and Strindberg's *The Bride* in November, both designed by Svoboda, who thus, under wartime pressures and shortages but perhaps with special incentive for that very reason, began his Prague theatre career. Within seven years he would be chief designer and technical director of the National Theatre, but that step was to be preceded by several shifts of regime, dozens of elaborate productions, and a number of critical personal decisions affecting his career.

One and a half years after the initial New Group productions, the war

2. An untitled, anonymous newspaper clipping dated 18 February 1942.
3. An untitled, anonymous newspaper clipping dated 9 May 1942.

and occupation came to an end. During that time, Svoboda continued his secondary-school teaching and occasional theatre work. Several proposed productions never materialized, and, in any case, all theatres in occupied Bohemia were officially closed during the last year of the occupation. People's efforts were concentrated on the sheer struggle to survive.

The end of the first phase of Svoboda's career may be considered as coinciding with the end of the war, in May 1945. At that point he had several options available to him: he could take advantage of his 1939 acceptance by the Philosophic Faculty of Charles University and pursue his original academic career; he could complete his architectural studies; or he could devote himself to full-time professional theatre activity. Characteristically he elected not one, but two of his options, the second and third, thereby postponing a final decision on his career. Nor did he abandon his interest in the liberal and fine arts other than formally: literature, history, music, and philosophy have remained part of his life and important sources of his creativity.

The period of 1945–50 involved Svoboda in several decisive events. It was a time of great ferment and artistic release, as a new generation tried to make up for the six lost years of the war and as the social and political life of the nation was approaching the crisis and bloodless coup of February 1948, when the Communist Party took over the regime of the postwar, second Republic and established the Czechoslovakian Socialistic Republic.

Along with several friends, including some from the New Group, Svoboda formed the leadership of a newly created major theatre ensemble, the Grand Opera of the Fifth of May, which moved into Prague's largest theatre (formerly the German theatre in Prague) after the war; in August 1946 he became its chief designer and technical director. In the meantime he began a five-year, university-level course of study in architecture at the School of Fine and Applied Arts in Prague. The combined responsibilities and their demands on time and energy took their toll: more than once, according to Svoboda, he was found slumped over his drawing board, virtually unconscious after prolonged stretches of sleepless work devoted to production deadlines and academic assignments.

In the Grand Opera of the Fifth of May (which despite its name also performed legitimate drama), Svoboda found the interim period of 1945–48 an especially fruitful one, during which he did some of his most creative early work, especially in collaboration with two of its directors, Alfred Radok (drama) and Václav Kašlík (opera). Both men represented a continuation of the Czech prewar avant-garde tradition (which in turn had been strongly influenced by such Russian avant-gardists of the 1920s as Meyerhold, Vakhtangov, and Tairov)—a tradition of wide-open, liberated, irreverent staging methods employing elements of cubism, constructivism, and surrealism, with a frequent though not invariable socio-political orientation. Svoboda's work with Radok and Kašlík during these years, as well as his work with Jindřich Honzl at the National Theatre, represented a second wave of these avant-garde tendencies.[4] Some of Svoboda's outstanding productions during the years 1945–48 were *The Tales of Hoffmann* (1946), *Káťa Kabanová* (1947), and *Revizor* (1948), all of which revealed his inclination toward a synthesizing, collage technique. *Tosca* (1947) indicated his mastery of monumental architectural scenic effects treated with high imagination, and *Rigoletto* (1947) was a notable early example of his recurrent theatre-within-theatre treatment.[5]

With the change of regime in 1948, all theatres, as well as industry and commerce, were removed from private ownership and nationalized. The arts became an official concern of the state and were provided with large subsidies; an extensive network of repertory theatres began to be organized and centrally administered. Part of the elaborate transformation involved Svoboda's theatre coming under the control of the National Theatre in the fall of 1948 as one of its three houses and being renamed the Smetana Theatre. Largely because both Kašlík and Radok went along with the merger, Svoboda transferred as well, even though it meant his stepping down to the position of deputy designer and technical supervisor under Josef Gottlieb, the chief at that time. Two years later, after Gottlieb's death, Svoboda moved into the position that he has held to this day, chief designer and technical director of the National Theatre in Prague—an incredibly demanding job in which his previously demonstrated talents for organization and leadership were to be fully tested. A few months earlier, in June 1950, he had completed his five-year schooling at the School of Fine and Applied Arts and thus became a fully qualified, degree-holding, professional architect.

The second period of his career again closed at a critical juncture: he had completed his architectural training and was about to face a new and major challenge in his theatrical career. A certain fundamental choice was

4. Honzl (1854–1953), one of the dominant prewar directors, continued his career in somewhat modified fashion after the war, becoming increasingly politically oriented and at the same time more conservative in his staging. It is especially interesting that Svoboda never worked with E. F. Burian (1904–1959), the most significant of the prewar Czech directors, who continued to direct until his death. Nevertheless, according to Svoboda, Burian exercised a powerful indirect influence on him, as he did on virtually all Czech theatre artists between 1930 and 1950. As Svoboda puts it, "By watching his rehearsals and productions, I learned how to direct lighting, how to provide it with a score." *

5. Svoboda's work was not immune from criticism, especially in some of the productions directed by Radok; their radical flouting of conventions frequently sparked considerable scandal and controversy. *Káťa Kabanová* was called a "cultural disgrace," the colors of the scenery in Prokofiev's *Masquerade* "drowned out the music," *Rigoletto* was accused of formalism, *Revizor* of being too intellectual and contrived. One of the more wry remarks on a certain Svoboda tendency (at least in relation to conventional standards of the time) was that, "It would seem that a brightly lit stage will soon become an almost historic event."

inherent in the situation, and a brief consideration of some of its conflicting elements is necessary for an understanding of Svoboda's subsequent artistic and professional evolution.

One of these elements was Svoboda's attitude toward architecture. Far more than a challenging technical discipline or a potentially profitable career, architecture for him became associated with life itself:

> Actually it's life, not an abstract discipline—an aspect of life, an organization of life, the groundplan of life. It consumed my interest. It requires the foresight of sociology and psychology; you have to know history and how to decipher it. You must be able to grasp relationships; architecture becomes a kind of puzzle of life that you have to solve. In the Renaissance it was considered the queen of the arts, a guiding discipline in relation to other arts and to life itself. *

Svoboda's initial attraction to a career in architecture was partially based on his belief that the new, socialistic regime would allow for maximum creativity in architecture in the service of society, that architecture would be free of the commercial, profit-making pressures and attendant compromises that he associated with the bourgeois capitalism of the Republic. Subsequent events, however, provided a degree of irony, for it soon became apparent that the cultural program of the new regime carried its own special pressures that worked against creative freedom. Whatever its original, theoretical values may have been, the quasi-artistic doctrine of socialist realism as applied to architecture resulted in a pattern of official, establishment-approved, monolithic works notable for their tastelessness and lack of imagination or artistry, a far cry from the ideal and artistic visions of a young architect. They formed, as the saying went, a "disgrace perpetuated in stone."

Svoboda, perceiving a relatively greater degree of artistic freedom in theatre—or, in any case, a lack of permanent evidence of artistic compromises therein, turned away with some reluctance from a career in architecture, per se, and for the time being devoted himself fully to his work at the National Theatre.[6] His architectural training and skill, however, were by no means wasted. They integrally enhanced his stage designing work, and they reinforced his insistence on precision, scientific thoroughness, and the technical as an instrument.

The third stage of Svoboda's career extended from approximately 1950 to 1956, the "hard" period of Stalinist dogma in socio-political life and socialist realist dogma in the arts. As practised in the Czechoslovakia of the early fifties, socialist realism in theatre meant official, unimaginative insistence on near-naturalism in technique and an optimistic, socially beneficial (i.e., socialistic) message. Experimental, expressive techniques were denounced as formalism,

6. One observation on this decisive event was that Svoboda became an *emigré* from architecture.

and deviations from or criticisms of the basic socio-political line were simply not tolerated, presumably for the general welfare of society. Few of Svoboda's approximately sixty productions during this period indicate an advance in his artistry; in effect, he experienced at least a five-year caesura in his growth. Exceptions did occur, perhaps two or three a year; a prime example would be the Radok directed production of *Jedenácté Přikázání* ("The Eleventh Commandment"), 1950, a work which contained in embryo the essence of the subsequent sensation of Laterna Magika—the integration of film and living actor. More typically, several productions were never allowed to be performed, and Svoboda did a relatively greater number of productions outside Prague, especially in the early fifties, in theatres where official pressure was not as marked as in the National Theatre. His work during this period is marked by technical mastery, impressive monumentality or effective folk realism—depending on the nature of the script—and a prevailing literalism.[7]

Two of his other activities during these years are worth noting: his organizational work at the National Theatre, and his teaching at the Theatre Academy. Impelled by what he calls an "aversion to dilletantism," Svoboda set himself the task of reorganizing and modernizing the total technical production operation at the National Theatre, gradually building up a staff of specialists, engineers, and technicians to raise the operation to a consistently professional level and to train new people to take over key positions. The scope of his task is suggested by the technical and operational staff of over three hundred; a workshop aggregate consisting of three carpentry shops, two costume shops, and one shop each for machines, hardware, fabrics, photography, and properties; and a repertory system that performs over fifteen different productions each month at each of three theatres and thus necessitates a different scenic mounting each night, with attendant problems of transportation and storage. Even more to the point, it means that any designer must work within a number of strict limits. For example, his settings must be readily erectable, strikable, and portable; he is not able to assume that once erected, the setting can remain on stage. In any event, the reorganizational work took up forty percent of Svoboda's time, "a relatively high proportion," as he noted, "but on the other hand an investment that provided a high return because in the past I had to give up . . . a good setting because of a shortage of equipment or workmanship of poor quality in the stage shops." *

7. Svoboda's work during this period was frequently criticized for its "inadequate social message," its "pointless descents to formalism"; especially revealing are the following excerpts from a review of a Radok-Svoboda production as early as 1949, *Chodská Nevěsta* ("The Bride of Chod"): "The ingenious theatrical ideas can't hide ideological holes and emptiness . . . an example of unprincipled cosmopolitanism. . . . A pretense at a folk drama that dangerously confuses the unaware spectator." On the other hand, Svoboda was usually praised in terms of "archetypal realism, documentarily precise," "stringently realistic," "beautifully realistic work completely rid of . . . 'expressiveness,'" and "faithful rendering of landscape."

His teaching at the theatre division of the Academy of Fine Arts in Prague, from 1952 to 1958, provided another sort of experience. He taught a course on scenography for directors, orienting them in principles of design and stagecraft. Current productions were discussed and analyzed according to practical considerations of design and staging; secrets of the "kitchen" were revealed to the future directors. In the informal atmosphere of these weekly meetings, Svoboda was able to provide an insight into principles of art and design that were officially unacceptable at the time. According to one of his students, later a successful director and playwright, he provided them with a sense of what theatre art and freedom of expression might be; at a time when the mere use of a black backdrop was condemned as both formalistic and pessimistic, such guidance was especially welcome.

The most rigid period of dogmatism began to loosen after the XXth Soviet Party Congress and the overt denunciation of Stalin by Khrushchev in 1956. General conditions did not change overnight, but at least relatively more room for varied production methods became available, and the narrow, restrictive guidelines of official policy became more flexible. Artists had more space within which to operate, and they were not slow to take advantage of the opportunity. Another major period of creativity was about to begin for Svoboda, one that carried him beyond the point he reached in the early postwar years. This fourth period of his career, one of particularly rich creativity, extended from the late 1950s to the middle 1960s, with no sharp break at either end. The beginning, of course, was marked by the post-Stalin general thaw. With the gradual unclenching of official controls, the other, positive side of a state-supported cultural program had a chance to reveal its potential advantages: money genuinely devoted to culture, large subsidies provided with no expectation of profit in return, guaranteed artistic employment. For Svoboda and the directors with whom he worked, it meant a steady underwriting of ambitious production programs on a long-range basis, with relative freedom from box-office pressures. Any such program has inherent problems, as became apparent—non-dismissable employees, a degree of bureaucratic control even under the best of circumstances, and a certain tendency toward complacency and "leveling"—but these difficulties were not intolerable for superior artists whose creative efforts relied at least in part on extensive budgets.

It was a good period for the Czech theatre as well as for Svoboda, a period, as Svoboda puts it, when the artists foresaw the wave of liberalization that began in January 1968. "An artistic potential existed in all fields, one that had accumulated under the suppression of freedom when ideas were compromised and couldn't be expressed. Artists, as well as other people, were forced to employ a secret language, to communicate in metaphors in order to tell people that there is more to existence than sports and creature comforts. This compression burst in Brussels."* Svoboda was referring to the Brussels World's Fair of 1958, where the Czechoslovakian pavilion became an unexpected success. "They proved a sensation because they were full of pressure and had their first real chance to show the outside world what they could do,"* he adds.

Besides receiving an award for industrial design, Svoboda received two other gold medals at the Fair for his share in the creation of two remarkable new entertainment forms: Laterna Magika and Polyekran. Both are discussed more fully in a subsequent section (p. 77), but here it may simply be noted that they employ a synchronous, multi-screen, multi-projection system of both slides and film, the Laterna Magika also employing a complex integration of living performers with screened images. Both forms created a sensation and made the Czech pavilion one of the most heavily attended at the Fair.

Three years later, in 1961, Svoboda won the grand award for scenography at the São Paolo Biennale international competition; his success there was followed up by his lecturing and guest designing in Brazil two years later.[8]

The fourth period of his career was also marked by the beginning of his joint creativity with another outstanding Czech director, Otomar Krejča, a former actor who, like Radok, also served an apprenticeship under E. F. Burian. Among the outstanding Krejča-Svoboda productions in Prague during this period were Hrubín's *Srpnová Neděle* ("A Sunday in August") in 1958, Topol's *Jejich Den* ("Their Day") in 1959, Chekhov's *Sea Gull* and Tyl's *Drahomíra,* both in 1960, and above all the productions of *Romeo and Juliet* in 1963 and *Hamlet* in 1965 (Brussels), in which Svoboda achieved at least a temporary peak in that phase of his work involving the interplay of space, architecture, and movement.

Equally satisfying at the beginning of the same period was Svoboda's work with his other favorite and long-time director, Alfred Radok, on Leonov's *Golden Carriage* and Osborne's *The Entertainer,* both in 1957. Their association had its most overt success in Laterna Magika, the product of their close cooperative effort, with Radok providing the direction and scenario. Because of complications and misunderstandings attendant on Laterna Magika's subsequent Prague production history, however, Svoboda and Radok parted company for a number of years in the early and mid-sixties.

Both Radok and Krejča are major artists, directors who create on a large scale almost of necessity, who are able to use Svoboda's design and technical contribution masterfully, with all stops out, in the service of the script. Svoboda is frank in admitting his need of significant directorial co-artistry; he

8. The Czechoslovakian representatives dominated the São Paolo competition for a number of years. In 1959 the scenographic award was won by František Tröster, and in 1963 by Ladislav Vychodil.

considers himself lucky to have had such outstanding people to work with as Radok, Krejča, Kašlík, and, earlier, Honzl—to name only those who have affected him most. These directors, and others, have extended his awareness, his "index," as he puts it, as a result of their respective approaches and special methods: Krejča, with his exhaustive analysis of a script, his large sweep and feel for an architectural, dynamic setting, can fill out a big production, but can also work most effectively on more intimate works; Radok is a more intuitive, romantic, perhaps capricious artist who puts greater emphasis on the special contribution of the actor and is more likely to strive for a near "magical" theatricalized effect. (It is worth noting that Svoboda's most special work with projection techniques has been done with Radok, whereas his most striking work with kinetic scenery has been done with Krejča.) In Kašlík, Svoboda respects the completely professional opera director, one who knows not only music but also drama, and who recognizes the positive, creative contribution that scenography can bring to an operatic production.

With all three directors, Svoboda feels a sense of association, of understanding and communication sometimes based on only half-articulated thoughts. His ideal would be to do virtually all of his work in Prague with such directors and with the first-rate technical staff that he has built up, in a cultural environment that he knows intimately in its pressures and rhythms. In other words, scenography is not a completely transportable commodity for Svoboda. Although he has clearly demonstrated his ability to produce with great success far from his native stages, there is no doubt that he feels most organically *right* in his homeland, with his long-time creative associates. Nevertheless, for a number of reasons, chiefly involving economics and availability of materials, Svoboda, despite his preference for working at home, ironically finds that during recent years he is more nearly able to actualize his artistry abroad, as the register of his productions at the back of this book will indicate.

In any case, the years between 1957 and 1965 formed a crest in Svoboda's creative output and brought him increasing international recognition. Among a host of offers to design abroad was his one assignment in America to materialize thus far,[9] a production by the Opera Group of Boston of Luigi Nonno's *Intoleranza* in early 1965, for which he employed a very ingenious variation of his projection techniques—the use of live television projection on a large screen simultaneously integrated with the stage action.

Svoboda's earlier experiments with lighting, stage kinetics, and special projections ascended to new levels of sophistication and complexity by 1965. Since that time, in his most recent period, he has refined still further on many

9. Several projects in America did not materialize, including a dramatization of *The Iliad,* intended for Lincoln Center in 1967, and *Salomé* for the Civic Opera in Chicago in 1968.

of these techniques, especially those involving lighting and projections, has done some of his most notable design work with technically rather simple but highly imaginative settings, and has devoted himself with more intensive speculation to the chronic problem of a new theatre space. With various notable exceptions, he has seemed more content with ripened and economical use of tried and mastered techniques than extravagant experimentation with new ones. A case in point was his first production with Radok after many years, an adaptation of Gorki's *The Last Ones* (1966), which, as he put it, "rehabilitated" the Laterna Magika principles after their commercial debasement by others and suggested the powerful artistic possibilities of the hybrid medium.

Both the Bremen (1966) and Prague (1969) productions of *Don Giovanni*, on the other hand, illustrated Svoboda's poetic, intuitive, highly metaphoric sense; both were technically uncomplicated; both gained their power from the poetic conceit that underlay their realization on stage. Much the same could be said, with obvious variations, of the London production of Chekhov's *The Three Sisters* (1967) as well as the Prague production of Dürrenmatt's *The Anabaptists* (1968). A number of outstanding productions were based on refinements of previous techniques in lighting and projection: associated with the use of a Svoboda specialty, intense low-voltage lighting, are *Tristan und Isolde* (Wiesbaden, 1967) and *Sicilian Vespers* (Hamburg, 1969); with a matured, lyrical use of projections, *Die Frau ohne Schatten* (London, 1967) and *Pelléas and Mélisande* (London, 1969); and with a starker, more graphic system of projections functioning as critical commentary, *Hra na Zuzanku* ("The Suzanna Play," Frankfurt, 1968) and *The Soldiers* (Munich, 1969).

Svoboda's theatre-related exhibition work has also continued, notably at Expo 67 in Montreal where he again helped to make the Czechoslovak pavilion one of the most popular with several projects, especially a dazzling new multi-screen, synchronized projection system known as Diapolyekran, which presented a highly imaginative short program, *The Creation of the World*.[10]

Additional honors and prizes testified to a growing recognition of his accomplishments. In 1968 he was granted his own nation's highest honorary artistic title of National Artist. In 1969 he received an honorary doctorate from England's Royal College of Art as well as the annual Sikkens Prize of the Netherlands, previous winners of which include such men as Le Corbusier. In 1969 he also had the honor of having his production of *The Flying Dutch-*

---

10. In the summer of 1969, Svoboda began work on a commission to design a special exhibit to open at Nuremberg, Germany, in March 1971 in celebration of the 500th anniversary of the birth of Dürer. Svoboda has been given a free hand to create a scenario, function as director, and, of course, design all technical elements. His intention is to create an audi-visual confrontation of the works of Dürer with 500 years of Nuremberg's subsequent history by means of mobile and fixed projection screens, live TV, and other devices within a two-story space of Nuremberg castle.

Preliminary sketches by Svoboda for the unproduced *Elektra*.

man open the Festival season at Bayreuth and be the season's sole premiere.

It is apparent that the freshness and variety of Svoboda's creativity show no signs of abating. If anything, his talents seem constantly to seek new or ever improving forms of expression. In a discussion of forms in art, Stark Young once observed, "What counts is this force of life as it goes discovering, creating, and fulfilling the forms that reveal and express it. By this a work of art is alive."[11] It is precisely this force of life that marks Svoboda's creativity, as it does his temperament. A man of medium stature, Svoboda gives an impression of restrained alertness, of energy banked and well controlled. Occasionally, Svoboda's manner may even convey an impression of mildness and a certain remoteness, but such impressions are superficial and finally misleading, for Svoboda is a man of glowing intensity once his interest is aroused and he warms to his subject. Then his features become animated, his eyes brighten, and his voice suddenly acquires added range and expressiveness. With a spontaneous, intrinsically histrionic flair he often proceeds to reinforce his verbal account with dynamic gestures and movements as he strives to communicate the precise, essential quality of a given production and the concept it embodies. Such moments reveal how deeply rooted in feeling and, indeed, passion is Svoboda's creativity, and how important a role the intuitive plays in shaping his art.

11. Stark Young, *The Theatre* (New York, 1954), pp. 57f.

Any consideration of Svoboda as a stage designer runs into a basic semantic problem: finding an appropriate term to describe what he considers his profession to be. He does not believe the English-American term "designer" to be adequate, and other general terms such as "bühnenbildner" or "décorateur" are even less satisfactory because, according to him, they all imply a person who conceives a setting for a play, renders it two-dimensionally on paper—perhaps stunningly—and then in effect retires from the field, having fulfilled his commission. Svoboda's concept of his work involves much more than this; hence his preference for the term "scenography":

> My great fear is that of becoming a mere "décorateur." What irritates me most are such terms as "Bühnenbildner" or "décorateur" because they imply two-dimensional pictures or superficial decoration, which is exactly what I don't want. Theatre is mainly in the performance; lovely sketches and renderings don't mean a thing, however impressive they may be; you can draw anything you like on a piece of paper, but what's important is the actualization. True scenography is what happens when the curtain opens and can't be judged in any other way.*

Similarly, he goes on to say, scenography is ever and always a means toward an end: "We aren't circus performers or stage magicians; we're theatre workers, and for us scenography is a *means* toward actualizing a play and not the opposite."*

It is not surprising, therefore, that Svoboda is less than enthusiastic about exhibitions of scene design which feature static, two dimensional preconceptions of a setting. He considers a scene design as merely a temporary aid that will undergo many changes before it is actualized. Only a final photographic record of the scenery on stage in production begins to be authoritative, and even that is ultimately inadequate, especially for most of Svoboda's work. For this reason, exhibits of Svoboda's work rely heavily on kinetic models, and he himself would prefer using films for exhibition purposes.

Returning to the basic problem of defining his work, Svoboda goes on to say:

> I'm looking for a word to describe the profession, not the person, the profession with all of the means at its disposal, with all its various activities and responsibilities in terms of the *stage* and the creative work done in close cooperation with direction, with special emphasis on the free choice of all available means, not merely the pictorial and painted. For example, scenography can mean a stage filled with vapor and a beam of light cutting a path through it.*

Most assuredly, part of the scenographer's responsibility is his knowledge of all the technical instruments and materials with which he works:

lighting, construction, mechanics, mathematics, optics. "A lack of familiarity with these elements simply means a restriction of creativity." In a larger sense, "scenography also implies a handling of total production space, which means not only the space of the stage but also the auditorium in terms of the demands of a given production." * Observations such as these clearly suggest the strong influence of Svoboda's own vocational training and architectural orientation.

Related to these basic issues are the specific approach of a scenographer to his task and also his relationship to the other elements of production, chiefly the directorial. Central to the first point, the approach to any given production, is Svoboda's basic pragmatism, his rejection of a priori theories or methods. As early as 1947 he expressed a fundamental principle:

> We don't promote any artistic discipline, that is painting, architecture, sculpture, as the central one. We synthesize—that is, we choose the artistic principle that corresponds to our theatrical concept. . . . Priority on the stage belongs to the theatrician and only then to the designer or director.[1]

Although Svoboda welcomes the potential contribution of the latest available techniques and devices and is able to derive maximum benefit from them, their use or non-use is really not essential:

> What is essential is the approach to the job: I would be delighted to create a setting of *cheese* if it best suited the play. You have to use expressive means that precisely *fit* the production concept. And that's where the true beauty of my work lies, for me. *

Svoboda has been criticized at various times for a seeming lack of consistency in his extraordinary range of materials, techniques, and approaches; the question of pinpointing a *style* to fit his work becomes a problem. His answer is characteristic: "Style is a matter of solving each work by the given conditions, which means not only consideration of the specific author, but also the given director, the theatre building itself, the main actor or actors: each element is unique, and you have to consider the features special to each one." * He then goes on to give an example: his prize-winning set for the Old Vic production of Ostrovsky's *The Storm* in 1967. After study of the text and consultation with the director, he prepared a design based on projections. But once he had seen the British company in rehearsal he threw out the original design, and made up an entirely new set of projections, simply because he perceived an incompatibility between his design and the performance the English actors were clearly going to give; the point is that he adapted his work to them. By the same token, as he is frank to admit, the relative heaviness or complexity of scenography also depends on the actors; for example, if he is to design a set

1. Svoboda, quoted in E. Bezděková, "Reportáž skoro pohádková" [An almost magical story], *Středoškolák* [The High School Student] (n.d.), p. 10.

Svoboda at his office desk under various posters advertising exhibitions of his work.

in which someone like Olivier will play the central role, he certainly isn't going to provide scenography that will in any way divert attention from a great actor who will clearly be the center of interest. Svoboda expresses the broader point in this way: "It's the law of theatre: theatre is a synthetic, componential phenomenon that ideally needs balancing—if it's short here, say in acting, you add there, in the scenography—or the opposite." *

On a more subjective level, one of the elements that enters into the given circumstances of a production for Svoboda is its context beyond the confines of the theatre: that is to say, the prevailing cultural mood or climate of the day, its socio-historical *moment,* and the response it awakens in him.

> It's easy to turn out routine designs and *études;* I can pour them out of my sleeve. But it becomes hard work when the project is meaningful. I like to put all that I know and feel of the world into a given work, and my biggest problem is when I can't find the right connection or establish a relationship with a work. I especially like to capture the flavor or scent of the specific time and place of a production; that is, not only in terms of the original script but also in terms of when and where we produce it. *

Svoboda's point here seems related to a more general observation: "Only that which is contemporary on stage can thoroughly interest the spectator and affect him strongly. . . . Contemporary art should present a ground plan of life, the life-style of its time." *

Svoboda's humanistic conception of architecture clearly applies to his conception of scenography; its ultimate significance is to be measured by its relation to human experience. Needless to say, it is not always possible to take significant socio-historical events into consideration; the nature of the external circumstances, Svoboda's schedule of production assignments, and the degree to which he and the director are attuned all affect the matter. Nevertheless, intangible and fugitive as this element may be, it can make the difference between a good production and a superb one. Examples of some productions that succeeded in expressing a genuine sense of their time, according to Svoboda, are *The Entertainer* (1957), *Romeo and Juliet* (1963), *Hamlet* (1965), *The Last Ones* (1966), and *The Anabaptists* (1968).

Still another example of the adaptability and range of Svoboda's approach, as well as what he considers to be the essence of scenography, is to be found in his projected version—as yet unproduced—of Goethe's *Faust,* with Alfred Radok as director. The production concept involves the dual identity of Faust's domestic servant and Mephistopheles; how to distinguish the two identities instantly becomes crucial. The setting would consist of a huge room virtually empty except for the thousands of books lining its walls. Svoboda's chief scenographic contribution would be invisible: a floor designed to produce either a heavy, hollow sound of steps or else absolutely no noise, depending on who walked on it and precisely where he walked. As Svoboda describes it:

> The servant walks to the door, and we hear the hollow sound of his steps in the vast room. He turns just as he reaches the door, and starts back—and suddenly—silence!—and we know, instantly, that it's the devil. Nothing is visible, but *this is scenography* and is what I think sets me apart from most other designers. It's scenography raised to scenographic *direction*.*

Above all, of course, scenographic work implies a very close tie with direction. As Svoboda puts it: "A good director is one who understands design, and a good scenographer can only be one who is also a director, at least in terms of his knowing the principles of blocking, movement, rhythms, and the expressive forces of the actor."* Svoboda feels that a good deal of his approach to a play is based on directorial principles, and he appreciates directors who are able to accept this approach on his part, just as he welcomes their ideas on scenography. When referring to the interplay of director, scenographer, and all the other elements of a production, he likes to cite the analogy of an orchestra; he sees scenography as one section of the orchestra, and the director as conductor: at times scenography will simply play along with the rest, at times virtually disappear while another section dominates, at still another time the scenography will, as it were, play a solo, and, finally, there are times when all the elements combine for a crescendo or grand finale.

When pressed, Svoboda admits that he must be able to agree with a director on the basic interpretation of a play, or else they part ways.

> But I'm open to persuasion and ready to accept the director's interpretation as better than my own—or else to go along with a director who wants to play it by ear—but I must be able to *accept* it and *make it my own,* very much like an actor and the interpretation of his role, in relation to the director.*

It is clear that Svoboda's approach to his profession is a highly flexible, pragmatic one, but one that nevertheless insists on certain principles, chief among which is the premise that a scenographer must be more than a designer[2] and that a theatrical production is an organic, existential process, the specific configuration of which will inevitably vary each and every time, depending on the given elements:

> The basic principle is what happens on stage, the quality of its rendering, its relation to the play, and whether the expressive means that were used are appropriate to the objectives that the director and designer agreed upon. The

2. In fact, Svoboda questions the wisdom of schooling that is specifically intended to produce designers or scenographers, as such. He believes that basic training in some other, broader, essentially more "philosophic" field is of greater value, one that would provide wider horizons, such as a sense for "the drama inherent in space, people, the occasion—stage 'details' are only secondary."*

Svoboda's model for an unrealized production of Jan Amos Komensky's *The Labyrinth of the World and the Paradise of the Heart.* The free-form panels were to move, to fold, to take projections; their shape was intended to suggest the human brain. Svoboda designed the stage for touring, hence the special construction.

question is whether they've managed to concretize their idea. This is the big issue. . . . Scenography must draw inspiration from the play, its author, all of theatre. The scenographer must be in command of the theatre, its master. The average designer is simply not that concerned with theatre.*

Experimentation and the Technical

Forming the background or, perhaps more accurately, the foundation of Svoboda's scenography, both at its boldest and its simplest, is his profound, scrupulous respect for the painstaking experiment and research that precede its ultimate appearance before the public. It is easy enough to appreciate the intricate calculations that lie behind Laterna Magika or the related Polyekran system and their derivatives, but even such seemingly artless productions as *The Sea Gull* or *The Entertainer* rely to a considerable degree on techniques or materials that can result only from patient, precise, truly scientific work in advance. Although many people, both critics and artists, sincerely believe that science, technology, and systemization are inherently hostile to art and creativity, Svoboda is most emphatically not one of their number: "My father, a carpenter, always told me that if you want to do something new, you first have to *command* the *old*." ° Svoboda has, if anything, a rage for order, for precision, for the laws that underlie his work because, as he puts it, "it means that the given element has been mastered and can be used as an instrument." ° His feelings about music are significant in this respect:

> I admire its order, its purity, its cleanness — this is what I would like to establish in scenography. I know it's impossible but at least I want to aim for it. I'd like to eliminate dilettantism and make theatre truly professional. Scenography is a discipline. . . . I've been pursuing an ideal for twenty-five years: precision, systemization, perfection, and control of the expressive means available to scenography, even the ordinary means. Why shouldn't this age make the most of its technical developments as previous eras did? that is, the machinery of the baroque era, the electric light at the turn of the century.[1]

It is precisely because of his efforts to approach the ideal of scenography as a discipline, as a systematic instrument, that Svoboda places such emphasis on experiment, which he considers as nothing less than a responsibility:

> What we're concerned with is method, its logical development: something which has disappeared from our work. A method can become exact only by the concrete solving of problems. Concrete problems are a necessary *étude*. No art can be satisfied with only theoretical solutions. . . . Principles arrived at in the past reveal nothing of the possibilities in today's solutions, and the passive employment of finished creations would mean artistic stagnation for the present. . . . Theatre means creating, seeking, experimenting.[2]

1. Although Svoboda's temperament and frame of reference in most respects vary significantly from those of Piscator and Brecht, his campaign for a theatre that truly reflects its age and its scientific spirit, in production techniques as well as in subject matter, echoes one of their favorite themes.
2. Svoboda, quoted in "Scéna v diskusi" [Discussion about scenery], *Divadlo* [Theatre] (May 1966), p. 3.

He is even more explicit in the following passage; his emphasis on the taking of risks may seem strange coming from the man who places such stress on scientific precision, but actually the two values go hand in hand in Svoboda's work:

> Experiment is an obligation. The sole means of regeneration for real creativity and a voluntary acceptance of risks. This applies with double force in theatre, because a theatre artist has never had and will never have the possibility of testing his experiment "uncommitedly" in some remote laboratory beyond the perimeter of the stage.[3]

One of the innovations introduced by Svoboda in his supervision of the scenic and technical operation of the National Theatre was an experimental laboratory or workshop precisely in order to provide the necessary research for effective experimentation.[4] In doing so, he appreciated the irony inherent in making the established National Theatre the home of experiment, rather than, as is more usual, confining experimentation to a marginal, semi-amateur studio. In short, the flow of innovation and its results has been from the establishment theatre to the small theatre, rather than the other way around as was the case before World War II. But Svoboda understands the reason for the reversal: "Today's stage experiment . . . can only grow from firm economic foundations, from a wide circle of co-workers, experts, and from financial security that provides at least relative thoroughness in the experimental process."[5] Svoboda's present staff includes specialists in chemistry, electronics, mechanics, and optics, as well as draftsmen and recent graduates of architecture.

Another avenue of experiment for Svoboda has been his exhibition work, which he frequently uses as a technical proving ground. Almost invariably, exhibitions provide larger budgets than those available for theatre production; in effect, Svoboda takes advantage of the money invested in the exhibitions to develop certain instruments or techniques, which he then brings back for use in the theatre. When ideas or materials have proved their worth before the public, the people in charge of theatre budgets are more likely to be persuaded to underwrite their use in productions. The Laterna Magika and Polyekran systems were a case in point, as was the more recent Diapolyekran in Montreal, which was subsequently used in two German productions by Svoboda in the 1968–69 season, *The Suzanna Play* and *The Soldiers*.

3. Svoboda, "Možnosti a potřeby" [Possibilities and needs], *Divadlo* (September 1967), p. 8.
4. The Scenographic Laboratory was founded in 1957 as part of the National Theatre's scenic and technical workshops; its immediate supervisor was Miroslav Kouřil, who had been E. F. Burian's designer. Subsequently, in 1963, the Laboratory, under Kouřil's direction, became an autonomous research and consultative organization known as the Scenographic Institute, an identity that it has maintained to the present.
5. Svoboda, "Možnosti a potřeby," p. 8.

Svoboda's attitude toward experimentation and a scientific foundation as necessary ingredients of scenography is closely bound up with his basic assumptions about the role of technology in the theatre. Two of his most well known statements on this issue are: "It all depends how you use technology: an electric current can kill a man or cure him. It's the same in a theatre production: the technical element can harm it or be used to help prepare a masterpiece";[6] and again: "Modern technical progress belongs in the modern theatre just as an elevator or laundromat belongs in a modern building."[7] Offsetting what may seem to be an excessive preoccupation with the technical in such statements, especially when they are taken out of context, is Svoboda's equally characteristic observation that the technical is solely a means: "My dream would be not to have it there; but I have to use it now because certain things would not otherwise be possible. In five years there may be other means and other results."[*] Perhaps most directly to the point is Svoboda's simplest assertion, "Knowledge of the technical makes creativity possible."[*] To continue the chain of reasoning, one might add that knowledge of the technical derives from experiment, and experiment is meaningful only when scientific or systematic. The example that Svoboda frequently cites of the relationship between the technical and the creative concerns some of his projection systems: not until the development of an electronic apparatus to synchronize a number of projection machines could Laterna Magika or Polyekran progress beyond its initial, limited stage.

A few other technical elements recurrently employed and frequently devised by Svoboda warrant at least brief attention, for they exemplify the kind of research and development projects undertaken by the theatre laboratories, and they figure prominently in some of Svoboda's most important scenographic work. One is a low-voltage unit which he has used to great artistic advantage in lighting many of his productions. Each lighting instrument has its own transformer, which makes feasible a much smaller lamp filament in conjunction with the reduced voltage. The resultant beam of light is more intense, "whiter," and more controllable than one cast by traditional units. The advantages of the low-voltage unit are especially evident in Europe's 220-volt system, for the drop in voltage allows for a proportionately greater reduction in filament size than would be possible in a 110-volt system. Two variants of the unit are what Svoboda calls the low-voltage lighting "thread," and low-voltage "sector lamps." The "thread," a unit with a lens, casts a beam of light

6. Svoboda, quoted in "Rozhovor o inscenačním stylu" [A conversation about production style], *Informační Zprávy Scenografické Laboratoře* [Informative news of the scenographic laboratory] (April 1959), p. 2.
7. Svoboda, "Nouveaux Éléments en Scenographie," *Le Théâtre en Tchecoslovaquie*, ed. Vladmír Jindra (Prague, 1962), p. 60. This booklet was published in French and Russian; my citations are translations from the Czech manuscript copy, but I am providing reference to the pagination of the French edition.

that remains essentially parallel and highly efficient (most lighting units invariably throw a cone-shaped beam); the unit found its optimal use in *Majitelé Klíčů* ("Owners of the Keys"). The low-voltage "sector lamps" are similar to the "threads" but their beams do have a slight spread; they employ parabolic mirrors but no lens, and are placed in units of six or nine each. They have been used extensively by Svoboda in such productions as *The Sea Gull, Drahomíra, Svätopluk,* and above all in *Sicilian Vespers.* Their effect is to create a curtain or wall of light; Svoboda sets them in a counter-lighting position, that is at an angle from high at the rear of the stage aimed down toward the front; in this way, they pass through a greater distance of air and thus create the maximum effect of light-as-substance. The effect can be heightened in certain circumstances, if desired, when the low-voltage units are combined with an aerosol spray, which of course makes the air much denser; when the extremely high-intensity light beam passes through such hyper-dense air, the result truly approaches the paradox of insubstantial solidity. The most striking use of the combination occurred in the Wiesbaden production of *Tristan und Isolde,* in which a column of light figured prominently.[8]

Film and slide projections are almost a Svoboda trademark; yet before he could employ them effectively to achieve his exceptional results, several peripheral problems had to be solved. For example, the basic problem with all projections on stage is how to project a clear and bright image while at the same time providing enough light for the actor or scenery in front of the projection screen; rear projection is only a partial answer. For a long time Svoboda assumed that the real answer lay in increasing the intensity of the projected image—that is, in the efficiency of the projection instrument. It was only after many years and a variety of experiments that he realized the answer lay in the projection screen, its color and reflectibility; subsequent research led to special screens developed for maximum reflection and minimum diffusion. Before the projection problem was adequately solved, however, a solution was required for the auxiliary problem of parasitic light—that is, the light reflected from the floor surface, which weakens the light and image on the projection screen. The answer lay not only in having a non-reflective, velvet-like covering on the floor, but in tilting the floor backwards at a slight angle, plus providing

8. The development of the aerosol technique is a saga in itself. The basic principle consists of a fine spray of droplets that form on the particles of dust that are so readily available in most theatres; the droplets are electrostatically charged to repel each other and thus avoid clustering and falling in a fine rain. The basic problem was that the stirred-up dust became a health hazard, but this was remedied by the addition of a medically-approved, throat-soothing liquid as the basis of the spray. A further problem became apparent almost at the same time, however; the unusually high degree of heat given off by the special lighting units evaporated the droplets much too quickly. This was solved by adding an oil emulsion to the droplets to offset the rapid evaporation. A final problem: how to get rid of the droplets once they had served their purpose? Solution: altering the electrostatic charge so that the droplets attracted each other, formed larger drops, and fell.

the floor with a slight series of lateral ridges; these combined measures, in conjunction with the specially developed projection screens, enabled Svoboda to achieve the effective interplay of screen and living actor that was essential to several of his major artistic successes, especially Laterna Magika and *Their Day*.

A list of similar technical projects could soon fill a sizable technical manual, but two very recent technical breakthroughs are worth noting. Although they were yet to be used in production at the time of this writing, Svoboda incorporated them in his designs for two specific productions during the 1969–70 season. In a number of previous productions Svoboda used mirrors in highly dramatic fashion, particularly in *Ze života hmyzu* ("Insect Comedy") and the Brussels *Hamlet*. He hoped to heighten their effectiveness by using newly devised *pneumatic* mirrors—mirrors whose reflective surfaces are bonded to a flexible material that by remotely controlled changes in air pressure forms either a convex or a concave surface. By this means the images seen by the audience can be radically reshaped. The device was originally intended for use in the Milan production of Prokofiev's *The Fiery Angel*. The other innovation involves laser beams and holograms: the formation of visible but incorporeal forms in space. These are, in effect, projections without projection screens, or projections in air: shapes or images that can be walked through but remain undisturbed and visible.[9] Svoboda intended to use this hardly credible innovation for the ordeal of fire and water in his production of *The Magic Flute* in Munich in 1970, but final technical matters were not perfected in time. He still plans to use laser beams for a new form of projection in this production, but he is putting off the combined use of lasers and holograms until the Munich production of Goethe's *Faust* in 1971.

Even this brief listing of technical devices should indicate the extent to which Svoboda relies on contemporary materials and techniques in his efforts to make today's theatre representative of its age; as things stand, according to Svoboda, theatre needs to catch up. In 1959 he wrote: "Stage technology has always dragged behind the general technical advances of the time . . . we're still at the luna park and merry-go-round stage as far as I'm concerned."[10]

Two additional points must be kept in mind in trying to make a proper assessment of Svoboda's exploitation of a whole range of technical elements:

9. The essential process begins when a laser beam is split by being partially passed through and partially reflected by a special mirror. Part of the original laser beam registers on photographic film directly (no camera or lens is necessary); the other part of the original laser beam is reflected from the object to be reproduced before registering on the film. In effect, the film "captures" two different focal points of the laser beam. A slide is made from the exposed film. When another or subsequent laser beam is passed through the slide, a three-dimensional image is produced, one which can be projected on a screen or else exist at a pre-determined focal point in space.

10. Svoboda, "Scéna přítomnosti a budoucnosti" [The setting today and tomorrow], *Ochotnické Divadlo* [Amateur theatre] (1959), 5.5:109.

he always conceives of such elements as *instruments,* as means to an end, not as ends in themselves. Moreover, he always conceives of them as organically related to the total production, as dramatically integral elements: "the technical is an organic, synthetic element; it acquires poetry and metaphoric power."* Nevertheless, one may still ask, why so much emphasis on the technical? One response is that, in fact, a great many of Svoboda's productions involve a minimal use of technical devices. Those productions that do employ a heavy complement of the technical usually manage to hide the fact, and even when they don't, their underlying intention is not to provide technical spectacle but to serve the production, to provide maximum expressiveness for the production concept.

Otomar Krejča, closely associated with Svoboda for over ten years as a director, sees Svoboda's relation to the technical from still another perspective: "What interests him above all is the effect of the scientific-technical eruption of our century on man. He is not only aware of but also respects the humanism, the cultural and philosophic relevance, of all of today's technicism, but he also sees its cruelty, folly, and monstrousness. He does not use the stage to propagate a technicized religion; his basic value is always the relation of man to man, the human equation: the ability of artistic talent to create an authentic new reality that testifies to more important discoveries about the human spirit than any technical characteristics may provide."[11]

11. Otomar Krejča, from a speech, the text of which was printed in *Zprávy Divadelního Ústavu* [News from the Theatre Institute], No. 8 (1967), p. 26.

Trying to classify Svoboda's scenographic mode as primarily symbolistic, constructivistic, expressionistic, cubistic, or even illusionistic is ultimately a fruitless exercise. The fact is that his work exhibits instances of each of these modes as well as combinations of them. What underlies all of his work, however— except the literalism or monumentalism of some productions during the Stalin era—is his search for the intangible essence of the work and his attempt to express it in the most appropriate manner, on the stage, in theatrical terms, which, for him, implies a synthesis of expressive elements.[1] Almost without exception, moreover, he sees *dynamism* as fundamental to any work of theatre art; if nature abhors a vacuum, Svoboda abhors a fixed, static stage, which strikes him as being a perversion of the essence of theatre. Quite inadvertently, perhaps, he approaches the Aristotelian position that regards *action* as the very heart of the drama; not action in the crude sense of the word, but in the sense that drama means responsiveness, change, and movement, when broadly conceived as ranging from a quiet, steady flow to abrupt, radical revolution. One of his relatively early recorded remarks on the subject is revealing: "A tree sways and trembles; it's a dynamic organism. That's why a setting can't be done naturalistically, because it's precisely the details of nature that can't be slavishly imitated. The naturalistic theatre is a corpse."[2] Putting the matter positively, he stated at another time:

> In the old theatre the scenery was erected and usually remained fixed without change throughout the entire scene. But what is fixed in the stream of life that we see represented on the stage? Is the room in which we declare our love the same as the one in which we scream curses? . . . That's why we abandon a static space with its restricted means and instead create a new one . . . more appropriate to the life-style of the present and the mentality of our viewers.[3]

In recent conversation, he reiterated this central principle:

> I don't want a static picture, but something that evolves, that has movement, not necessarily physical movement, of course, but a setting that is dynamic, capable of expressing changing relationships, feelings, moods, perhaps only by lighting, during the course of the action.*

1. Svoboda would not even reject a mode that seems hopelessly out of date: "The problem with painted scenery was not that it was painted, but the way it was painted. The descriptive realism of the nineteenth century has its place in history, but not in today's world and not in today's theatre. . . . But if the entire performance and the entire creative team that thinks through and prepares the performance came up with a concept based on a painted scene and provided it with a unified principle revealing new 'laws' that we're unaware of at this point, there might be tremendous results." Quoted in Jaroslav Dewetter, "Před objektivem" [In front of the lens], *Divadlo* (1962), 3:26.
    2. Svoboda, quoted in "Rozhovor o inscenačním stylu," p. 2.
    3. Svoboda, "Nouveaux Éléments," pp. 59f.

The last phrases are very important, for it is all too easy to assume that Svoboda is obsessed with sheer movement, an assumption that is somewhat encouraged by the term "kinetics" that has been applied indiscriminately to his scenography in general. As he likes to point out, perhaps only thirty of his more than 330 productions have involved material, tangible movement. But most of his productions, if not indeed virtually all of them, have indeed employed a subtler form of kinetics that accompanies the action as an expressive, responsive reinforcement, most often, perhaps, by lighting: "lighting as a dramatic component, not merely illuminating the scene or providing atmosphere."* Kinetics, in short, is a matter of the given production: both of his *Hamlet* productions, his second *Insect Comedy*, and his latest *Dalibor*, for example, have all employed variations of a physically kinetic stage; *Their Day* and *Soldiers* depended on kinetics via projections; but *The Sea Gull* and *The Three Sisters* have relied solely on subtle, suggestive changes of lighting to accompany their action.

"Suggestive" is perhaps as close as any single term can come to describing the fundamental scenographic effect that Svoboda seeks. This is to say that he steers clear of both illusionism and alienation; instead, he would rather prompt the viewer's imagination. In this as in so many other respects, Svoboda avoids extremes, instinctively preferring to reinforce and vivify the theatre's traditionally evocative, inherently metaphoric power with as much leeway as possible in the specific scenic mode that would seem most relevant for a given production. What remains constant, however, is Svoboda's conviction that the setting must not foreshadow the action or provide a summary illustration of it; it is as if he were allergic to a setting, no matter how impressive otherwise, that seems to announce the heart of the play in one brilliant image: "Theatre means dynamics, movement; it is a living thing; therefore, scenography should not be fixed and tell all at once, as expressionistic design tends to do."*

The setting should evolve with the action, cooperate with it, be in harmony with it, and reinforce it, *as the action itself evolves*. Scenography is not a background nor even a container, but in itself a dramatic component that becomes integrated with every other expressive component or element of production and shares in the cumulative effect upon the viewer. And it is precisely in order to heighten the expressive, responsive, and dynamic power of scenography that Svoboda so often draws from the whole range of technical instruments and materials that he is able to handle so masterfully. In the hands of a lesser artist, many of the technical elements employed by Svoboda would become extraneous and cumbersome, and would call attention to themselves. Indeed, it sometimes happens that even Svoboda is unable to achieve complete success in integrating the technical with the spine of the action, but in the great majority of his productions he has the imagination and sheer command of his medium to be able, not only to add scenography to the other elements, but to *fuse* it with them and thus form a total artistic, dramatic, and above all theatrical entity that has far greater power than the sum of its parts.

It is, of course, an essentially imaginative, poetic process, one that demands an innate capacity for synthesis and metaphorical thinking. Svoboda's perceptive statement on the essential character of a modern theatre production suggests the extent to which he possesses this capacity:

> . . . the individual elements [of production] are becoming more precise and . . . tending to join in a new, more polyphonic creation, in a multi-branched composition possessing several levels of significance among which a dialectical and contrasting oscillation develops, as much in the resultant theatre work as a total creation as in the individual scenes, situations, and characters, because a theatrical work is a stream of artistic images and a refined projection of their ideas far more than a tangible product. Because the point above all is the communication of a poetic message, not mere information.[4]

It is likely that one of Svoboda's basic tendencies—a metaphoric, imagistic, collage-like scenography (*The Tales of Hoffmann, Wastrels in Paradise, The Last Ones,* for example)—is related to his association with Alfred Radok, with whom he has done so much work on the integration of film and stage. In any event, a certain orientation toward the techniques of the film medium is evident in remarks like the following:

> We're at a disadvantage in relation to film; we can't use rapid cutting techniques or enlarged details; we always have to work with the scene as a whole. We manage to create focus and tension by a *contrapuntal accord* between action and props, movement, sound. . . . Modern directional methods call for an open, free stage; it can't allow itself to be bound by a static ground plan; the setting has to become adaptable to the action without strain and instantly.[5]

Actually, something more fundamental to Svoboda's sense of theatre is involved here. He is fond of illustrating his concept of the very essence of theatre by referring to a single chair set on the stage, as a result of which the chair already acquires a new and special identity; it does so all the more when it is lighted in a certain way, and especially when it is then juxtaposed with other objects. Such objects may in themselves be quite banal, but when imaginatively placed and illuminated, they may reveal new aspects of their being and perhaps even their poetry. It is this highly charged potential—this "contrapuntal accord" in even the most ordinary of theatrical configurations—that Svoboda loves and that forms the basis of his inherent sense of theatre.

Still another indication of the imaginative, poetic cast of Svoboda's approach is evident in the following remark:

4. Svoboda, "Možnosti a potřeby," p. 7.
5. Svoboda, quoted in Dewetter, p. 27.

Each of these [scenographic] elements must be flexible and adaptable enough to act in unison with any of the others, to be their counterpoint or contrast, not only to project a two or more voiced parallel with the other elements but to be capable of *fusing with any of the others to form a new quality.*[6]

Svoboda, like most artists, is not much given to theorizing, especially about his own work. Nevertheless, he has thought through the interrelationship of his premises, principles, and methods to the point of formulating a relatively abstract but clear set of statements that amounts to an aesthetics if not a metaphysics of his work. The following set of statements is significant in several ways: in providing a rationale for the main line of Svoboda's prodigious creativity, in clearly suggesting not only the scope of his talent but also its complexity, and in relating him implicitly to the central stream of what could be called the modern scenographic tradition (i.e., Appia, Craig, the Russian avant-garde), while at the same time indicating the distinct evolution of that tradition in his work.

> ...the relationship of scenic details, their capacity for association, creates from the abstract and undefined space of the stage a transformable, kinetic, dramatic space and movement. Dramatic space is psycho-plastic space, which means that it is elastic in its scope and alterable in its quality. It is space only when it needs to be space. It is a cheerful space if it needs to be cheerful. It certainly cannot be expressed by stiff flats that stand behind the action and have no contact with it.[7]

The goal of scenography cannot merely be the creation of a tangible picture ... and in itself [scenography] is not a homogenous totality. It separates into a series of partial elements, among which certainly belong form, color, and also tempo, rhythm—in a word, the elements that are at the disposal of an actor. And it is precisely by means of these elements that the scene enters into close contact with the actor, becomes capable of dynamic transformation, and can advance in time just as the stream of scenic images created by the actor's performance. It can transform itself synchronously with the progress of the action, with the course of its moods, with the development of its conceptual and dramatic line ... the elements that possess this dynamic ability are, first, space and time, and then rhythm and light ... elements that were revealed for scenography by Craig, Stanislavski, and Appia. They are intangible elements and they indicate the essential characteristics of scenography. And, if Craig, Stanislavki, and Appia simply referred to these elements as space, time, rhythm and light, then we today must speak of them as dramatic time, dramatic space, and dramatic light.[8] And if these elements were positivistically lined up next to

6. Svoboda, "Scéna v diskusi," p. 2. Italics mine.
7. *Ibid.*
8. In one of his later works, *The Work of Living Art,* Appia made use of terms that went beyond merely space, light, color. He referred, instead, to living time, living space, living color, which more nearly anticipate Svoboda's dramatic time, and so on.

each other in a row, then today they enter into synthesis. First of all space and time in order to form time-space, the fourth dimension of the stage, in order to overcome their traditional antithesis and replace it by the duality of matter-immaterial energy, which is precisely as real as any tangible object on the stage, and the visible manifestation of which is movement. Dramatic movement implicates space and time. And thus the translational movement of the elements completes the circle. According to my judgment, that's the utmost point and highest degree of scenic development that it's possible to achieve at this time: the combined action of the parts reveals the dynamic principle of the entire system, which is characterized by the intermeshing of configurations that continuously form and dissolve.[9] The goal of a designer, according to this premise, can no longer be a description or a copy of actuality, but the creation of its multidimensional model. That's what I tried to accomplish in the productions of *Their Day, Owners of the Keys, Drahomíra,* and *Dalibor,* and then primarily in the production of Čapek's *Insect Comedy* and Shakespeare's *Hamlet* in Brussels, and in Gorki's play *The Last Ones.* The basis of a theatrical presentation is no longer the dramatic text, but the scenario, the evidence of the fusion between direction and scenography, and their aiming toward a common goal.[10]

These extended quotations have the virtue of placing the easily misunderstood kinetic principle of Svoboda's scenography in proper perspective. The purpose of Svoboda's stage kinetics, whether physical and overt or subtly intangible (i.e. lighting), is not a mere theatrical *coup,* but the formation of what he calls *psycho-plastic* space: three-dimensional, transformable space that is maximally responsive to the ebb and flow, the psychic pulse of the dramatic action. The underlying premise is the belief that theatre is distinguished from all other arts precisely by what Svoboda emphasizes as its intangible forces: time, space, movement, non-material energy—in a word, dynamism. And it is precisely to the enhancement and intensification of this end that all of Svoboda's technical resources are dedicated.

Equally illuminating in the cited material is the conception of the scenario as a working script that integrates the dramatic text with expressive stage directions and dramatically functional scenography. This Craigian vision of a union of scenography and direction has approached reality in the close co-creative work of Svoboda and directors like Radok and Krejča. It is obviously a concept that demands not only great individual gifts and skills but also a true fusibility of temperaments and creative methods.

9. In many places, but especially here, Svoboda's creative concept is strikingly akin to that expressed by Coleridge in his classic definition of the Imagination: "It dissolves, diffuses, dissipates, in order to recreate. . . . It is essentially vital, even as all objects (as objects) are essentially fixed and dead." *Biographia Literaria,* Chap. XIII.

10. From a speech by Svoboda, the text of which was printed in *Zprávy Divadelního Ústavu,* no. 8 (1967), pp. 28–29.

Both the concept of the scenario and that of psycho-plastic space imply a highly responsive, flexible, expressive theatre that is built on the principle of synthesis, not only between the various elements of scenography but, in a larger sense, between scenography, direction, acting, and dramatic text. The final, materially all-inclusive element yet to be considered in Svoboda's total concept of scenography is the theatre building—more precisely, the enclosed space that contains all the other elements.

> I hope to design and construct a theatre in which we can truly create during rehearsals, in which we can improvise the building of dramatic space, and only then, secondarily, worry about constructing the necessary *décor.* We need a theatre in which we can create psycho-plastic space by means of flexible elements; the ideal is that not only the stage but the entire theatre becomes an instrument on which an artist can play.* [1]

Before elaborating on Svoboda's ideal theatre, it is interesting to note that of all the existing forms of theatre structure (specifically, existing forms of stage-auditorium relationship), Svoboda somewhat ruefully prefers the proscenium form. If conditions were different, he would prefer the three-sided form of Chichester or Stratford, Ontario; but as things are he finds such theatres too inflexible because they are not able to transform their space for different productions. "They are not yet an instrument for varied tasks; they are still a cembalo rather than a piano."* Moreover, as a chief limitation, they are incapable of becoming *frontal,* which Svoboda finds necessary for many productions: "certain plays are written with a certain space in mind; sometimes you *want* the proscenium theatre, deliberately."* For essentially the same reasons, Svoboda is even less enthusiastic about the arena or central staging form; his reasoning is indicative of the traditional side of his theatrical orientation:

> Ancient plays had a known, familiar ceremony and ritual; the spectator didn't have to see as much in order to participate. But Chekhov, Hellmann, and others, their plays are not designed for this—all the spectators need the same view, need to share a common communication. Arena means that each person has a different experience, receives a different message.*

To put the matter in another way, the proscenium theatre space, as inadequate as it is in many ways, still approaches the needs of today's production methods more closely than do its alternatives. "This," says Svoboda, "is a fundamental dilemma."[2] The dilemma is a painfully ironic one for Svoboda,

1. Svoboda's metaphor of theatre as instrument is, of course, a familiar one, and not restricted to designers. Eugene O'Neill, for example, speaks of "the instrument (the theatre as a whole) on which one composes." Cited in Lee Simonson, *The Stage is Set* (New York, 1932), p. 118.
2. Svoboda, *Zprávy Divadelního Ústavu,* p. 31.

for although most of his greatest work has been done within (if not because of) the limitations of the proscenium form, he would obviously prefer to employ his inventory of materials and devices in a totally different space than is now available to him. He has put the matter with notable frankness:

> Most of my devices and what I do with pictorial techniques are intended for what I hope will be the theatre of the future. At present they are still far from what I want; I still use them as decoration in the baroque, proscenium theatre, and it offends me to do so. The auditorium space and sight lines of the old theatre ruin me; they force me to radical experiments that sometimes result in mere spectacle; they are bad and go against my convictions. Many of them are simply improvisations forced by outmoded theatres.*

In other words, "the baroque theatre was true to its day in terms of its values, methods, and materials; it was contemporary *then*. But today that same architecture still dominates our theatre, *as if* it were contemporary."* And that is why Svoboda's ideal theatre would be one in which there would be no architectural division of stage space and auditorium space. Instead, there would be a totally flexible space which Svoboda calls "production space," by which he means a transformable configuration of stage *and* seating space according to the production concept most appropriate to each work; it is the concept of psycho-plastic space applied to the theatre as a whole. This, to Svoboda's mind, would be a theatre true to its day, as the baroque was true to its day.

Svoboda's ideal theatre does not yet exist and is not likely to exist in the near future. His own ideas about it are not spelled out to the point where they can be set down in blueprint form, nor are the instruments and materials that he thinks necessary yet readily or commercially available; moreover, the necessary funds for launching such a project are lacking. For all these reasons, Svoboda, ever the realist when it comes to such matters, prefers not to make fanciful sketches or models that cannot be actualized. Nevertheless, he has at different times expressed a sufficient number of basic ideas about such an ideal theatre to enable us to form a reasonably clear impression of its dominant characteristics.

It is significant, for example, that Svoboda does not ignore its cultural, social context. It would be a relatively small theatre with a seating capacity of not much more than five hundred. Furthermore, ideally, it would be designed for a specific director and ensemble: "a theatre should evolve from a specific group with specific features and aims and values, not as a result of administrative, official decrees."* At the same time, the theatre should be capable of subsequent evolution; but in no case should it be approached as a permanent, established institution.

A certain area of the theatre ought to be designed to function as a transition between the everyday world and the theatre's production core, an area that would provide "a caesura between the entrance of the visitor into the theatre building and into the production space, a pause that would facilitate his shift from visitor to spectator . . . as necessary for the theatre as the transformation of actor to dramatic character."[3]

The *production space* would be based on the principles of modules, entities capable of certain functions:

> They would be mobile and able to join in various combinations so as to form a transformable, psycho-plastic space. Moreover, they would also be self-contained energy sources (electrical) and function as lighting instruments. And they would have the further capacity of carrying other objects on and off with them.*

The modules would be flexibly related to an electronic gridwork or plugboard, and the total would form one powerful electro-mechanical apparatus designed for the more complete realization of production ideas by making possible various arrangements of stage and audience. The nearest analogy to this module system would be the Diapolyekran system employed by Svoboda at Expo 67 in Montreal, and subsequently adapted for his Munich production of *The Soldiers* in 1969. Central to both was a system of mobile cubes which functioned as projection screens with built-in projectors; some of the cubes in the Munich version had the added capability of functioning as mobile stages or acting areas. Both systems were, of course, primitive beginnings in terms of Svoboda's ideal theatre modules, especially in being limited to the stage (the audience space was unaffected), but they do indicate the direction of his vision. Another analogy would be a great, mechanized film studio designed to film a stage drama; that is, a sufficiently large space with virtually infinite possibilities in terms of lighting and projection as well as stage-audience arrangement.

A feature that would most certainly be essential to such an ideal *atelier*, as Svoboda calls it, would be the use of small, specially designed components to take the place of traditional stage machinery, which, except for its labor-saving function, Svoboda regards as virtually dead weight in the modern theatre: "an absolutely useless investment without a glimmer of imaginative potential."[4]

Svoboda's most recent general attitude toward such an ideal total theatre space again suggests the essential balance of his thinking:

> It may seem utopian but it is practical in that I know exactly what I want it to do. And it's important to remember that it can be used to create traditional theatre forms. It is not a *total-theatre* in the Gropius sense; in fact, it might

3. Svoboda, "Možnosti a potřeby," p. 10.
4. *Ibid.*

Svoboda and the noted Czech director Otomar Krejča in Svoboda's Prague studio in the fall of 1970. Between them is Svoboda's model for the *Oedipus-Antigone* production on which they collaborated during the 1970–71 Prague season.

take the form of a series of little baroque theatres: perhaps we might construct several stages and seating areas and have an audience of less than three hundred that would move to a different stage after each scene. And finally, we would of course not be restricted from doing very simple things. . . . It would ultimately become a generally used thing. Fifteen years ago my contra-beam lighting units were an innovation; now they are generally adapted. In other words, some aspects of this theatre might be special and solely applicable to it, but others would be taken over by theatres generally.*

A fundamental question relating to any ideal theatre concerns the dramatist. As envisioned by Svoboda, it is not a self-sufficient artistic organism;

it is, as he emphasizes, an instrument. Moreover, it is not an instrument to be used solely by the scenographer or even the director. It should be used by the playwright as well, used in the active sense of his designing his works with this sort of theatre in mind. Part of the problem in any theatre, Svoboda believes, is that most playwrights are ignorant of the theatrical means available to them; or, to put it another way, the theatre, especially one such as that envisioned by Svoboda, needs texts that allow or indeed demand the range and variation of scenography which it makes available. "Texts," of course, is not the best term, but rather "scenarios," a word which in its fullest sense implies an organic, cooperative creativity among author, director, and scenographer—a creativity, moreover, at least part of which occurs during the rehearsal period with the actors, in a theatre space that evolves into a specific production space during the total creative process.

It is this final vision, poetic in its very nature yet grounded in an exploitation of the technical—thus reflecting the creative duality of his own temperament, conceiving of theatre as a medium of fullest synthesis and devoted to making that medium responsive and expressive in the highest degree—that most aptly defines the career of Josef Svoboda at this point in its evolution.

Providing energy for its future course is an inner tension between his satisfaction, indeed happiness, with the traditional theatre and its techniques, even the oldest and simplest ("I don't reject the old techniques of theatre, I respect them; they may have a purpose in a given production; they are of the theatre. I'm happy to work in a limited, old theatre and do simple designs. I have a love for it"*) and what he calls his "restless spirit, from childhood," that inner force that compels him toward breakthroughs and new frontiers, toward what remains to be discovered, not only through new materials and techniques, but through what he calls "the great secret and mystery of space— the next five years may decide crucial matters affecting space in the theatre. It would be a great thing, even if it meant suppressing or rejecting my entire output up to that time."* It is ultimately his profound dissatisfaction with the traditional theatre, his desire to transcend it and achieve some new form, different in kind, that is likely to continue impelling Svoboda's creativity into the uncharted future.

PART II.
REPRESENTATIVE PRODUCTIONS ILLUSTRATED

Neither chronology nor order of importance forms the basis of grouping the following annotated illustrations. I have attempted to arrange them so as to provide a reasonably clear and thorough survey of Svoboda's main artistic and technical achievements. For this reason, several productions are sometimes grouped together, and at other times a production is presented by itself.

Two of Svoboda's observations are relevant to any examination of illustrations of his work:

> There is a danger in seeing pictures of my productions. All of the elements in a production tie in with each other and are truly dynamic, so that no picture can truly capture them with fidelity, even if no overt or material movement is involved.*
>
> There are two basic errors of criticism: the senseless mania of searching for previously used elements in new productions: the real question is whether the work is alive or dead, has an effect on the viewer or not. Equally erroneous is the idea that every artist, in fact every production, has to arrive with completely new revelations.*

An Introductory Survey

The following section is devoted to numerous examples of Svoboda's work, some early, some recent, some marked by a dominant scenic image, some by special scenographic techniques, others by variations on a similar theme. They do not display Svoboda's craft at its most striking or complex, but they do provide a useful introduction to the essential components that have characterized his scenography since its beginnings: poetic creativity, theatrical intuitiveness, and technical mastery.

Several productions illustrate Svoboda's use of a single, powerful scenic image to represent the essence of a given work. Rarely, if ever, does such an image remain either static or merely visual; that is, it usually alters its shape or composition in response to the action, and it is usually functional in one or more ways rather than a mere element of *décor*.

Figs. 1–3 Svoboda's first work after the war was also his first opera and his first major Prague production, *Kunálovy Oči* ("Kunala's Eyes") by the Czech composer O. Ostrčil (December 1945). As the photographs illustrate, the set consisted of a massive, austere, temple-like structure that was placed in various positions to correspond to the basic turns of the plot.

Figs. 4–6 Another of Svoboda's early works was his first encounter with a Janáček opera, *Káťa Kabanová* (based on Ostrovsky's *The Storm*), which was performed in Prague in January 1947. The production is one he remembers very fondly, and his remarks on it provide another example of his creative process, especially its synthesizing character:

Figures 1–3. *Kunala's Eyes.* One monumental scenic element dominates stage space in three different ways.

Figure 4. *Káťa Kabanová.* The basic tree unit placed on a turntable and starkly silhouetted against the sky cyclorama.

Figure 5. A shift of the turntable, the fence, and the lighting creates a new effect.
Figure 6. *Káťa Kabanová.* Still another shift of the turntable reveals the blending of exterior and interior, the realistic and the deliberately theatrical. Note the shadows cast on the "sky."

Figure 7. Macbeth. A blue-black scaffold stage enclosed by blood-red curtains and disintegrating walls reinforces the murderous action of the play.

There was no distinct interior or exterior, but one basic idea: I saw the characters as related to or moving in a tree, and so constructed a huge tree that could be walked on. It was supported by columns and posts so that the interior was formed by the space under the tree; that is, the tree roots, covered with ikons, establish the interior. The ancient tree became a space for playing, a space for acting. The effect was almost surrealistic, yet had a realistic basis in terms of Russian practices with ikons.

Exteriors were played on the tree, and by putting a fence on the tree we were able to suggest a bridge; there was also some action around the tree. Moreover, the tree was on a turntable and could be placed in different positions, thereby acquiring different aspects of reality; constant but always subtle changes were possible—kinetic stage effects. The interior and exterior blended with no sharp division between the two. Many differences were also established by lighting: when the interior was not important, it was simply played down, subordinated, largely by changes in lighting. The set offered great possibilities for projections, as well: the lighting instruments were placed so as to cast shadows of the branches as well as impressionistic color past the branches onto the cyclorama. And at the end, when Káťa leaps into the river, the cyclorama slowly slid off to the side to reveal a stage depth of blackness. The effect was typical of the entire production, which was done metaphorically, poetically.*

Fig. 7

A recent production of *Macbeth* in Prague (June 1969) also reveals a focus on one dominant scenic element that is both symbolic and instrumental, in this case a platform that suggests both a stage and an executioner's scaffold, and, indeed, functions as both during the play. On the one hand it ties in with

Figure 8. Ivanov. The photograph can only faintly suggest the symbolic juxtaposition of bark-covered fence and the velvet plush that covered virtually all interior objects. The contour of the fence also suggested elements of a Russian skyline, such as onion-shaped church towers.

some deliberate theatre-in-theatre effects in the production, and on the other hand it is the site of the multiple murders that punctuate the play, including Macbeth's final execution at the hands of Macduff. Intensifying the impact of the blue-black platform are the totally red, velour-covered surfaces that surround it: floor, monolithic walls, and curtain fronting the platform. The wall itself contributes to the drama in still another way: it gradually disintegrates during the course of the action, chunks of it being removed during numerous scene changes.

Fig. 8

One of Svoboda's more recent projects, Chekhov's *Ivanov* (Prague, February 1970), demonstrated his sensitivity to scenic materials and textures and their symbolic use. According to Svoboda, "the production was based on the contrast of two materials, rough-hewn, unpainted wood with the bark still on it, which formed a fence encompassing the entire scene, and a vibrantly green plush velvet material that covered both floor and furniture."° The wood was a valid epitome of the external environment: late 19th century provincial Russia. And the plush velvet covering connoted the essence of the domestic interiors: an oppressive, queasy-making, bourgeois spirit pervading the action and infecting the characters.

Figs. 9, 10

One of Svoboda's recurrent scenic devices is the mirror, which he employed both before and after its illustration here in Mozart's *The Magic Flute* (Prague, 1961). The slightly distorted mirrored surfaces functioning as walls, ceiling, and floor created startling alterations of space and a marvellous fictive, theatrical world. Svoboda mentioned still another purpose for the mirrors: "You can't escape the feel of the Rococo period in the music. The mirrors were

Figure 9. The Magic Flute. The triangular pattern of mirrored surfaces breaks up space and creates multiple fantastic images.

Figure 10. The Magic Flute. The addition of a ceiling piece adds still another dimension. Some of the mirrored surfaces reflect the rococo embellishments of the eighteenth-century theatre auditorium itself. Note the vertical triangular pieces at the left of both photographs.

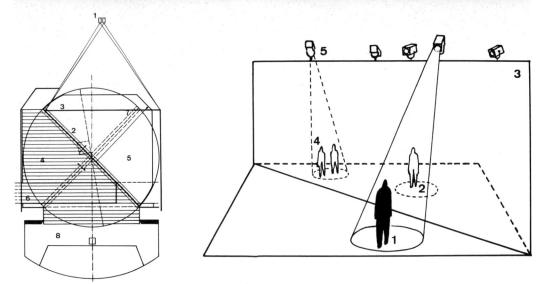

Figure 11. Groundplan of *The Wedding*. 1—Rear projectors: two slide projectors, 5,000 watts each; 2—mirrored wall, 50% transparent; 3—rear projection screen; 4—acting area at stage level; 5—raked acting area, 10% incline; 6—movable wagon stage; 7—position of mirror for second half of the performance; 8—forestage.

Figure 12. Frontal diagram of *The Wedding*. 1—Actor in front of mirror; 2—mirror image of actor, which may be replaced by another live actor behind the mirror; 3—50% mirrored screen (transparent mirror); 4—actors behind the mirror; 5—lighting bridge.

used to reflect period objects off-stage in the wings—flats, props, and so on. Also a ballet off stage, which normally might disturb or get in the way of stage business."*

Figs. 11–13

A considerably more sophisticated mirror technique was employed in the Berlin production of W. Gombrowicz's *The Wedding* (1968). Here the mirror was semi-transparent and extended the full width of a larger-than-proscenium turntable (Figure 11). The action of the play concerns a soldier at the front who shifts between reality and illusion, past and present. Both states were captured by the special employment of the mirror in conjunction with flexible lighting. "For example, we could place a table and chair behind the mirror, plus another chair in front of the mirror, and align them in such a way that the frontal chair seemed part of the rear arrangement, as well as being isolated in front of the mirror. The actor, in short, could be placed within his family circle while also still remaining solitary. The actor could be *transplanted* from reality to dream, and back again."*

Two productions, performed within less than a year of each other, reveal certain interesting similarities in Svoboda's embodiment of a basic dramatic theme, especially one that he can respond to personally. Both a modern Czech play, *Mlýn* ("The Mill"), by Z. Mahler, and Mozart's *Don Giovanni* have fate or destiny as a strong thematic element. Svoboda himself has distinct feelings about fate or determinism in events; he refers to the significant Brussels experience (see pp. 9–10) in terms of the sense of freedom and release he felt

Figure 13. The Wedding. The protagonist experiences one of his visions. Real actors appear behind the mirror, and are themselves backed by a rear-projected image.

there, and also to an almost mystic sense of the relationship of all things: "I felt that all things are connected, related, as if part of the same pulse or blood-stream, and that even the *things* we encounter have an influence on our decisions, somewhat fatalistically. It became an *idée fixe*." *

Fig. 14   Svoboda's scenography for *The Mill,* produced in Bratislava in May 1965, stressed the element of fate in the play and established a pattern that later appeared in the Bremen production of *Don Giovanni.* All the scenic objects and props, mostly everyday items, were arranged haphazardly at the rear of the stage and were moved into place as needed, quite openly and in a theatrical manner. "These objects," as Svoboda explains, "created a fated space, just as man's actions in certain situations create certain, fated consequences. The scenery became an actor in the drama, not merely a description of locale." *

But the overpowering scenic moment was saved until the end of the play:

> At the end the scenic objects formed the wall of a firing squad: a culminating, poetic effect—all the objects from life massing together as a backdrop for the end of life. And we were prepared for this absurd collage of a firing squad wall by the theatrical manner in which the objects had been handled throughout the play. We could accept the ending as fated. *The wall held the entire significance of the play.* Ordinary, routine objects arranged in various relationships to create poetic, metaphoric insights—that is what I love in theatre, what is unique in theatre, what sends chills down my spine. It's not a matter of truth but of a higher reality, something *ur*-natural in its very simplicity. This sort of

Figure 14. The Mill. The setting is based on an accumulation of everyday objects that are shifted by the actors and finally form a deadly wall.

theatre will never die, but always be. There can never be *no* theatre; it's part of humanity, existence, and culture.*

Figs. 15, 16   The subsequent Bremen production of *Don Giovanni* (January 1966) was externally influenced by two factors: the unusual depth of the stage in the Bremen theatre and the relatively low budget that Svoboda promised to work with (to compensate for a very expensive *Carmen* production he designed there earlier in the season). Both factors actually contributed to the effectiveness of Svoboda's scenography. His basic scenic image or device was a huge chess set; specifically, two chess boards ranged in the depth of the stage. The similarities to the production of *The Mill* then became apparent:

> All the props and furniture were stacked deep in the rear of the stage; at the beginning, the pieces formed the impression of a town, and then came apart. The individual pieces were not in the shape of chess pieces, they were realistic and natural; but they were *moved* like chess pieces. As if in a game of chess, the pieces began to move into pre-determined positions, certain pieces for each scene. Once the scene was over, the pieces were removed (all the movement being handled by members of the ballet). Finally, one piece was left—the

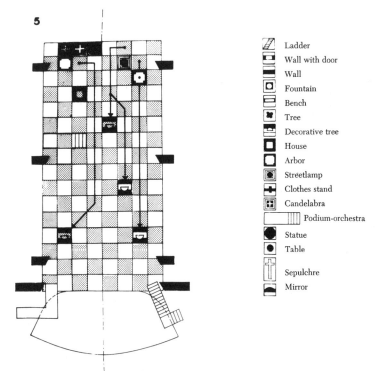

Ladder
Wall with door
Wall
Fountain
Bench
Tree
Decorative tree
House
Arbor
Streetlamp
Clothes stand
Candelabra
Podium-orchestra
Statue
Table
Sepulchre
Mirror

Figure 15. Don Giovanni (Bremen). A groundplan of the stage showing one set of the fated moves of the scenic pieces during the action; hundreds of such moves had to be planned in advance.

Figure 16. Don Giovanni (Bremen). Svoboda's model of the set indicates the depth of the stage as well as parts of the set extending over the orchestra pit.

Figure 17. The Three Sisters. Act IV, an exterior, lauded by critics for its evocation of shadowy autumnal woods by means of the stretched cords and special lighting.

Figure 18. The Three Sisters. A close-up of one of the window frames placed between two layers of cords.

Commendatore's statue. It was brought all the way to the front. Giovanni was checkmated. The whole effect was very suspenseful and theatrical. I mapped out every move precisely, a terrific labor that had to be figured out step by step with the music, and all of this had to be done in advance of rehearsals.

Why the chess image? That's something for which I have no clear answer right now; sometimes it takes me years to discover the point of a set, in that sense. Certainly, it had something to do with the manipulation of fate, each action having certain pieces assigned to it. Something to do with the law of opera plus the laws of games, or chance. Drama, like chess, has its precise logic and laws. Something about the idea of pre-determination attracts me; everything done has an influence on what follows, one act calls up another; a chain reaction is no accident. Giovanni kills the Commendatore; a stupid act, but his fate becomes settled.[*]

Three more examples of special scenographic elements or techniques devised by Svoboda deserve at least brief mention and illustration.

Svoboda has used the scenic device of stretched cords on more than one occasion, but probably never as successfully as in the London production of Chekhov's *The Three Sisters*, directed by Sir Laurence Olivier (July 1967). The cords were strung tightly from the floor up to the flies, more often than not in several layers. Scenic objects and furniture were sparsely placed in front of the cords, and window frames actually in between two layers of cords.

Figs. 17–19

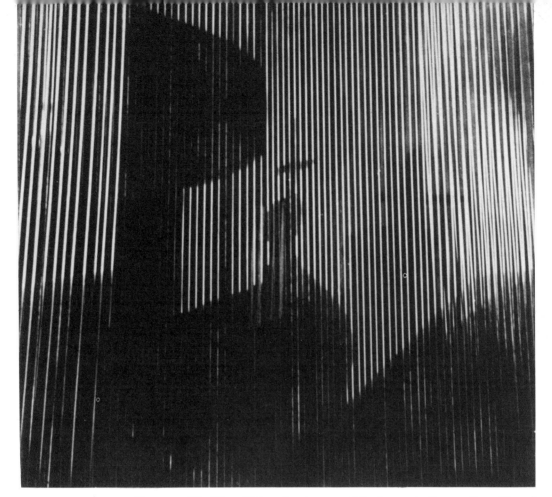

Figure 19. The Three Sisters, showing one of the few projections on the setting of strung cords.

Depending on how the cords were lit, from the front, rear, or above, they formed the impression of a solid wall, delicate bars, or shimmering depths without precise limit. Occasionally, also, some projections were used on the cords, for example the suggestion of buildings, but projection was a limited element in the production. According to Svoboda, the use of cords was related to an attempt to achieve a sense of "never-endingness," something that is reached for but impossible to touch, thereby of course reflecting a central theme of the play. More precisely, however, the starting point, the key to the scenography, were the windows:

> Windows are very special things in Chekhov; the thoughts and desires of the characters fly out through the windows, but life and its realities fly in the other way. The windows must be created by means of light, like that of the French impressionists—light dispersed in air. And this was captured by the strings in

Figure 20. Svoboda's rendering for Prokofiev's *The Story of a Real Man,* an interesting combination of stretched strips and curved planes. Projections were used on the strips.

front of and behind the window frames: light streams in from behind and in a different relation to light from the front; the shifting balances add to or lessen the sense of reality and dream. Originally, I tried scrim, but cords finally solved the whole problem, starting with the windows, but working for the entire set and all the scenes. The final result is *style:* the windows lead us to all of Chekhov's atmosphere. The interiors are not bordered or limited, but diffused.*

The set was eminently successful, a splendid actualization of the underlying production concept. Olivier said, "It was exactly what I dreamed of." In the course of time, however, the technical execution of the subtly arranged and designed lighting cues became slipshod; the necessary freshness and artistry of the technical accompaniment was lost. Svoboda has nothing but contempt for the school of theatre technicians to whom running a performance is a matter of routinized numbers, counts, and points. "I urged Olivier," he

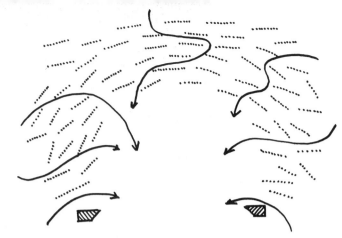

Figure 21. Svoboda's model for *Yvone,* one of the latest examples of his use of stretched cords or strips. One hundred twenty-five miles of dyed cord was used in this production.

Figure 22. *Yvone.* Svoboda's groundplan sketch illustrates the placement of the cords and possible paths through them.

says, "to have it dropped from the repertoire or else to have special rehearsals to bring the production back to where it belonged." [*] His point is twofold: the finest setting must always be supported by the technical, but the technical cannot afford to become merely routine.

Two variations of the stretched cord technique are worth at least brief mention. Prokofiev's opera *The Story of a Real Man* (Prague, 1961) featured strips three centimeters wide in different planes and at different angles. "They took projection decently," [*] according to Svoboda.

W. Gombrowicz's drama *Yvone* (Berlin, 1970) illustrated the complex evolution of the technique. The scene was enclosed by layers of stretched cords two millimeters thick, spaced one and one half centimeters apart. The cords extended a depth of some twenty feet in twelve layers and were dyed a vivid green, thus creating "an indefinite space, a green fog." [*] The striking effect was intensified by a floor covering of artificial grass turf of the same color. Svoboda considers the technique of stretched cords or strips a good example of "a principle that can be worked in various ways to create new expressive effects. Many of my basic techniques are never finalized, but continue to evolve and thereby underlie my entire work." [*]

Svoboda's setting for the Prague production of *Tosca* (May 1947) was a definitive example of monumental architectural scenery deliberately distorted in construction:

> I aimed at a more direct, less experimental, dramatic creation of more or less static space embodying a stifling baroque quality. The basis was a deliberately distorted perspective, created plastically, and designed to be practicable. The atmosphere was one of repression by church and nobility, a lack of freedom

Fig. 20

Figs. 21, 22

Fig. 23

Figure 23. Tosca. A two-dimensional, painted perspective of the sky in the background accentuates the distorted, oppressive mass of the church.

Figure 24. The Eleventh Commandment. The first actual use of the Laterna Magika principle. The cinema screen in the background was in ironic interplay with the live action on stage. Frequently the same characters appeared in both places at the same time, as can be seen in this illustration of the young man.

Figure 25. Straying. The tubular elements of gauze represent the formations inside a cavern, in which a group of adolescents become lost.

Figure 26. Straying. A transparent projection screen formed the rear of the stage. The images cast on it by rear film and slide projectors were to represent the actual word in confrontation with the symbolic straying of the youngsters lost in the cavern. The gauze tubes created an interesting effect of multiple layers and varied texture.

that can be felt in the music itself. Only one scene used a painted perspective, of heaven; it was appropriate in terms of representing the real sky of freedom, in contrast to the castle. The total set created a great dramatic effect; it was the first set of mine to be applauded at the opening of the curtain.*

Fig. 24

The operational ancestor of Laterna Magika was the Prague production of *The Eleventh Commandment* in June 1950, a musical version of an 1880s play by Nestroy, directed by Alfred Radok, and updated to the turn of the century. It was the first joining of theatre and film by either Radok or Svoboda. Only one screen was used, but its use was synchronized with the play of the actors.

It was the full Laterna Magika principle except for technical sophistication. Unlike the Brussels production, moreover, an actual play text was used as the basis of production here. A movie was made especially for the production, but it was meaningless without the actors on stage, and vice-versa. The play was produced in the film studio theatre, and we had the further advantage of their doing the expensive film work and loaning us projection equipment for the film, which was used throughout the play. A piquant fact was that the critics were not aware of the significance of what was done, which was typical of the critical level of awareness of the time [the peak period of pedantic socialist realism].*

Figs. 25, 26

Anticipating even *The Eleventh Commandment* as a forerunner of Laterna Magika was a Czech play that was never produced because of wartime censorship, J. Karnet's *Bloudení* ("Straying"). Svoboda worked on the project in 1942–43; in fact, Svoboda hoped to direct the play and therefore drew up a scenario for it. "I wanted to use what later became the Laterna Magika principle," Svoboda says, "but it remained only an idea because necessary techniques and equipment were not yet developed. Visual images of the stage and of external reality were to be placed in new relationships and create new dramatic elements and a new theatrical reality. The idea reached partial realization in 1950 [The Eleventh Commandment] and full realization in 1958, with Laterna Magika at Brussels."*

Fig. 27

Several productions that shared a theme from Greek tragedy illustrate the range and adaptability of Svoboda's scenography. For a production of *Hrdinové v Thébách Nebydlí* ("No More Heroes in Thebes"), a modern adaptation of *Antigone* presented in Prague's tiny Balustrade Theatre (November 1962), he designed a simple but powerfully expressive set based on an all-white cube. No curtain was used; instead, the audience faced a blank wall before the beginning of the play. Then the play began and the wall retreated—space was revealed as it would be if a cork were pulled out of a bottle. The wall moved silently and unobtrusively, on wheels; it stopped a few feet behind the end of the side walls, thus allowing room for entrances and exits on either side of the stage. Sometimes the wall moved forward and backward during the action, but always parallel to the curtain line. The few items of necessary furniture were pre-set in the surface of the floor and were raised and lowered as needed.

Fig. 28

An elaboration of the same principle was evident in Svoboda's plan for an unproduced version of Sophocles' *Elektra*, which was to have been performed in Rome in 1965. The piston-like rear wall is here supplemented by a

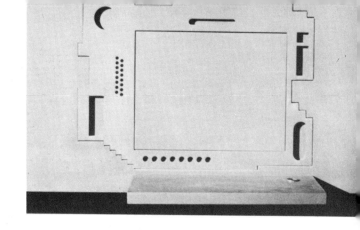
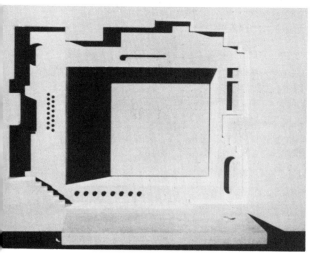
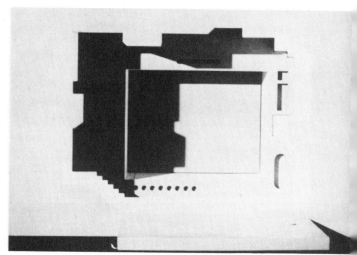

Figure 27. No More Heroes in Thebes. A stark, white set featuring a pistonlike rear wall that moved upstage and downstage during the course of the play.

Figure 28. Svoboda's mechanized model for *Elektra*, showing three of the set's many possible configurations. It is interesting to compare the scenography of this kinetic setting with that of the Brussels *Hamlet* (Figures 142–144).

similarly moveable, three-dimensional frame of irregular outline. Each unit could move separately or in conjunction with the other.

Figs. 29–31   Simpler in principle, but very well suited to play and theatre building was Svoboda's set for a production of Sophocles' *Oedipus* in Prague's largest theatre, the Smetana (January 1963). The setting consisted of a vast flight of stairs the full width of the stage, starting in the orchestra pit and reaching almost out of sight, which prompted one critic to describe the effect as "a sense of space without beginning or end and reaching from the chasms of the underworld to unseen heights—from primordial myth to time still to come."[1] The

1. Jan Kopecký, untitled review in *Rudé Pravo* [Red justice], 19 January 1963.

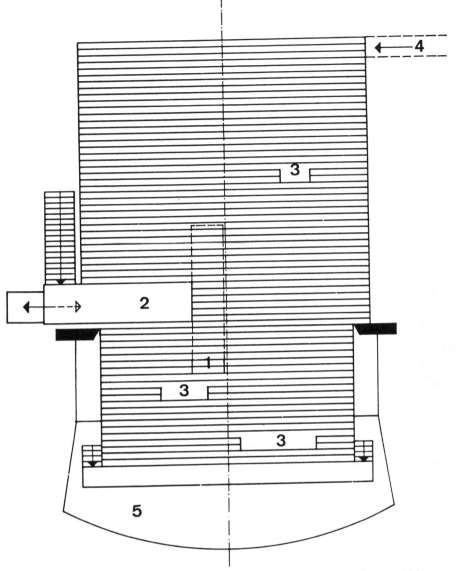

Figure 29. Oedipus, showing the groundplan of the giant staircase and its special features. 1—a practicable platform that could be thrust out or withdrawn under the stairs; 2—a practicable platform that could move laterally across the entire width of the stage; 3—fixed acting platforms; 4—entry connecting top of stairs to fly gallery; 5—orchestra pit.

stairs were occasionally punctuated by flat resting places that thrust out from the stairs themselves.

At the end Oedipus was left alone. Virtually all the flat levels disappeared. He climbed an endless staircase, into sharp counterlighting. Ideally, I would have preferred an inclined plane rather than stairs, but I had to have them because of the actors. In other words, the stairs were not crucial; I wanted the audience to forget their presence.*

Figure 30. Oedipus. The title figure is seen on platform no. 3, with platform no. 2 behind him.

Figure 31. Oedipus, showing the final scene of the play. An orchestra accompanied the action from under the stairs. In order for it to be heard properly, the risers of the stairs were made of acoustically "transparent" material similar to that found on the front of many loudspeaker enclosures.

Figs. 32–34   The Edinburgh production of Smetana's opera *Dalibor* (August 1964), provided a classic example of Svoboda's dynamic concept of stage space in a materially kinetic form. The setting consisted of two rectangular towers, each placed off-center on adjoining turntables, thus allowing for a virtually infinite variety of spatial relationships for the many scenes of the opera, and no loss of time for scene shifts. Indeed, the movement of one or both of the towers was often rhythmically integrated with the music. The basic device of rotating towers was supplemented by several asymmetrically placed projection screens in the background, and projections were also occasionally used on the towers themselves. The massiveness of the towers and their inexorable movement contributed to the power and magnitude of Smetana's music and the romantic tragedy of the libretto.

Figs. 35, 36   A later variation of the scenographic principle in *Dalibor* was to be found in Svoboda's set for Verdi's *Il Trovatore* (E. Berlin, December 1966). Instead of adjoining circular turntables at stage level, the basic device consisted of two overlapping, rotatable squares slightly above stage level. Each had a tower citadel placed off-center, representing the fraternal struggle at the core of the opera. Additional scenic variety was provided by a rectangular acting board behind the squares that operated on a see-saw principle and by a rear wall with a craggy relief surface, which, when illuminated by angled lighting, provided numerous dramatic effects of highlights, shadows, and color.

Figure 32. The Edinburgh production of Smetana's *Dalibor*, indicating the combination of rotatable towers and rear projection screen.

Figure 33. Dalibor, showing the towers on adjoining turntables and their twenty-four different positions.

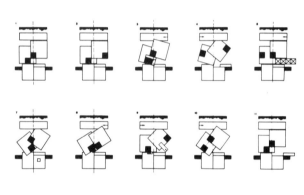

Figure 34. Dalibor, the finale—no projections, but strong low-voltage counter-lighting.

Figure 35. Groundplan of *Il Trovatore*, showing the varied positions of the rotatable squares and their tower citadels for the different scenes of the opera.

Figure 36. Two views of Svoboda's model for *Il Trovatore*. The frontal view clearly reveals the angled rear acting board (tiltable) and the dramatic relief surface of the rear wall.

Figure 37. An Optimistic Tragedy. The setting and stage space were determined by two surfaces variably slanted in relation to each other, with the top surface occasionally receiving simple projected images. The bottom unit was on a turntable.

The Theatre of Light

A number of Svoboda's productions may be studied in terms of his evolving use of light for the creation of space as well as atmosphere. A brief survey of some representative productions based primarily on lighting as the key scenographic element reveals progressive refinement in Svoboda's scenic principles, as well as in the technical elements available to him.

Fig. 37

Svoboda has frequently made use of a wedge-shaped arrangement of planes which, illuminated in various ways, creates visual and spatial effects far beyond the possibilities seemingly offered by its components. As early as 1957, in the Prague staging of Vishnjevski's *Optimistic Tragedy*, Svoboda demonstrated the almost limitless spatial possibilities offered by two surfaces slanted toward each other against a plain black background. In this case, the lower surface was a slightly raked stage turntable containing necessary scenic objects; the upper surface was an asymmetrically shaped flat capable of as-

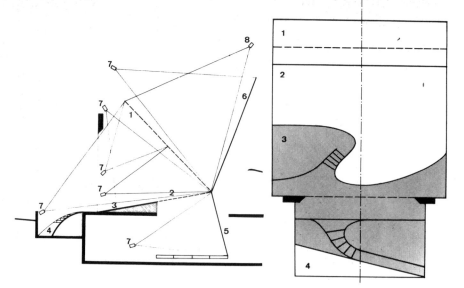

Figure 38. A Sunday in August, side elevation. 1, 2—scrim projection surfaces; 3—fixed acting platform; 4—orchestra pit; 5, 6—opaque projection screens, diffusive surfaces; 7—frontal slide projectors; 8—rear slide projector.
Figure 39. A Sunday in August. Groundplan.

suming various angles in relation to the floor. Simple projections were used on the upper flat to heighten the sense of open sky.

Figs. 38–40 A marked refinement on this technique was evident in the Prague production of an original Czech play by F. Hrubín, *A Sunday in August*, in April 1958. Svoboda described the scenography this way:

> A sky made grey by the hot summer air, and the motionless surface of a pond were here created by projections (front and rear) on the surface of two large flats that met each other horizontally at an angle of forty-five degrees, with a thoroughly diffused light being formed near the line of their meeting. This method produced a visual impression of unusual depth on a stage that was actually quite shallow, as well as a great sense of the surface of water.[1]

The actual technical arrangement was more complex than Svoboda's description suggests. As the diagrams reveal (Figures 38 and 39), four projection surfaces were used, two of them of variably transparent scrim (Numbers 1 and 2) forming an angle of forty-five degrees and two others of opaque material (Numbers 5 and 6) backing up the first two at obtuse angles. Each of the surfaces had at least one projector assigned to it alone, and the potential variety and subtlety of spatial visual effects was enormous.

The scenography of both productions—*An Optimistic Tragedy* and *A Sunday in August*—depended primarily on the skillful and imaginative use of lighting, per se; although projections were employed, their function was essentially supplementary.

1. Svoboda, "Nouveaux Éléments," pp. 65f.

Figure 40a. A Sunday in August.

Figure 40b. A Sunday in August.

Figure 40c. A Sunday in August.
Figure 41. The Sea Gull, Svoboda's rendering.

Figure 42. The Sea Gull, Act II, exterior.
Figure 43. The Sea Gull. The entire set was enclosed in black drapes; the branches, a unifying element, remained fully visible throughout the play.
Figure 44. Svätopluk, suggesting the stark simplicity of the setting and the powerful effect of counterlighting and minimal scenic elements.
Figure 45. Svätopluk. The curtains of light combined with the light-reflecting material of the costumes to create special effects of space and color.

Figs. 41–43

Svoboda's development of special low-voltage lighting instruments led to still richer expressive possibilities from lighting alone, virtually without the aid of projections. The Prague production of Chekhov's *The Sea Gull* (March 1960) was a striking early example. A basic scenographic element consisted of clusters of leafy branches that evoked the natural surroundings of a lake and unified the four scenes of the play. A review of the production noted one of its chief characteristics:

> The newness of the handling of space results from the lighting, which creates an atmosphere of silver-greyness that envelops and yet also penetrates the entire area, so that one almost forgets the fact that everything is being played within black drapes . . . or perhaps you think that the stage is enveloped in scrim, but this is a scrim that is woven by low-voltage lighting units concealed behind the branches. We see beams of light but think of them as sunlight streaming through the leaves. What persuades us is the coloration of the light — its sheer whiteness, which is the chief mark of spectral differentiation of this new, low-voltage illumination.[2]

Svoboda described his own approach to the problem in a brief statement:

> The production of *The Sea Gull* presented us with the challenge of creating a summer garden in full sunlight in such a way that this light, the heat, and the dense atmosphere of a summer day on stage would have an actually physiological effect on the viewer. We reduced all the possibilities that offered themselves for the creation of this atmosphere to a stage enclosed in black, a basic curtain of light in the proscenium frame angled toward the audience (thereby creating an equivalent for the traditional scrim), and an additional ten curtains of light placed variously in the depth of the stage, each one only five to seven feet wide. The "curtains" are formed by specially constructed, low-voltage lighting units placed in strips and concealed by fragments of tree branches; the resulting picture of a garden and its atmosphere is evoked simply by the penetration of "sun" light through the branches of a tree.[3]

Figs. 44–46

A fuller, more absolute use of the low-voltage curtain or wall of light marked two scenographically similar Prague productions, a contemporary opera on legendary material, *Svätopluk* (April 1960), and a classic Czech drama, *Drahomíra* (June 1960). Svoboda's remarks on the former apply to both works: "The modern music and the fact that the work was being produced by the National Theatre led to the rejection of all traces of naturalism and the stressing of high stylization. The technical conditions themselves, given by the sheer number of performers and the complexity of the musical demands, led us to strip the stage of everything not directly involved in the action. . . . We were successful in exploiting the possibilities of low-voltage

2. Miroslav Kouřil, "Československá scenografie," *Informační Zprávy Scenografické Laboratoře* (May 1960), p. 134.
3. Svoboda, "Nouveaux Éléments," pp. 66, 68.

Figure 46. Drahomíra. A suspended scenic element conveys a sense of massiveness without disturbing the open, free quality of the set. Both *Drahomíra* and *Svätopluk,* like *The Sea Gull,* were played within black drapes.

lighting and ordinary light sources to create curtains of light that have an absolutely physiological effect on the viewer—without his becoming aware that the rear and sides of the stage are covered by nothing more than black drapes."[4]

In another article, Svoboda added further details:

4. Svoboda, "Scénický textil v opeře, *Svätopluk,*" *Informační Zprávy* (June 1960), pp. 147f.

To a great extent we solved the problem of scenic space in both . . . by the use of curtains of light. For both, we divided the stage into five planes demarcated by strips of light placed across the entire width of the stage. Transversely, the stage was divided into three sectors, so that we were able to organize dramatic space here directly by changing the walls of light (just as in *Hamlet* [Prague, 1959] we organized it by the movement or reflecting panels). An important element in both of these productions, in which we used the same technical construction for the light sources, were the costumes, which helped create the sense of dramatic space in conjunction with the changes in the value and intensity of the lights; the surface of the costumes caught the light and reflected it into space, and their color created the desired scenic atmosphere.[5]

Fig. 47

Recent technical advances in materials and instruments, especially abroad, have provided two further examples of Svoboda's creative imagination in the use of lighting. The aerosol technique (p. 24n), used to enhance the visual effect of low-voltage lighting beams, achieved vivid results in the Wiesbaden production of Wagner's *Tristan und Isolde* (December 1967). Svoboda's setting was based on a spiral platform set inside a cyclorama created by tightly strung ropes, onto which semi-abstract projections were cast.[6] In the center of the spiral, however, Svoboda managed to create a seemingly substantial column, or circular curtain, of light.

Figs. 48–50

Even more gratifying to Svoboda was the success of his production of Verdi's *Sicilian Vespers*, in Hamburg (May 1969), during which he reached at least a temporary peak in his creation of space by light. No projections at all this time, and no assistance from aerosol; only, as he put it, "clean kinetic architecture and clean light achieved the desired purity and point of this production." * Improved technical equipment led to curtains of light significantly more effective than those employed in any of his previous productions.

> The scenography of the production was an example of pure architecture: flights of steps that are divided into sections that move laterally, supplemented by circular walls that rotate into the scenic area along with the movement of the stairs. But the main element was the diffuse light that created a kind of foggy ambience for the steamy Sicilian scene, the broiling sun and sweltering climate. The effect was that of light as a substance, light materialized, resulting from the special new lighting instruments that we designed. I think that we achieved a new level of lighting technique. And I think that Appia and Craig, especially, would have marvelled at the outcome. *

5. Svoboda, "Nouveaux Éléments," p. 68.
6. The use of strung ropes recalls a similar technique in the London production of *The Three Sisters* (July 1967), and the Prague production of Prokofiev's *The Story of a Real Man* (April 1961).

Figure 47. Tristan und Isolde. A vivid though insubstantial column is created by high-intensity light and Svoboda's especial aerosol technique.

Figure 48. Sicilian Vespers, a production that Svoboda esteems for the advanced and pure state of its two dominant scenic elements: lighting and kinetic architecture.

Figure 49. Sicilian Vespers.
Figure 50. Sicilian Vespers.

A notable offshoot of Svoboda's recent work with lighting has been a variety of experiments with color projection in the creation of stage space, experiments which hearken back to the relatively simpler scenography of *An Optimistic Tragedy* and *A Sunday in August* (Figures 37–40). The result of the later experiments might be called colored space or spatial color; in either case, the emphasis is on a three-dimensional use of color, primarily through the use of expressive surface forms and impressionistic projections. Svoboda sees his work in this area in terms of two main types, the first of which may be illustrated by several productions beginning with *A Midsummer Night's Dream* (Prague, 1963).

Figs. 51, 52

Svoboda's scenography for Shakespeare's *Dream* employed several expressive elements, chiefly a series of leaf-shaped cutouts hit by colored light and projections. "The leaves, golden on one side and black on the other, were suspended in different planes and at different angles, thus enabling the actors to move *within* the projections rather than *against* a cyclorama. These leaflike projection screens could be variously folded or tilted and, if necessary, removed from the scene entirely." * This key element complemented the more stable part of the set, a raked floor that curved up at the rear to form a cyclorama-like wall (Figure 51). The construction was of horizontal metal grating covered with wooden lathes. Three leaf-shaped disks could tip out from the floor to provide entrance space for the elves.

The lighting was based on two principles. The space behind the special rear wall and under the floor was counter-lighted, thus projecting light rays through the spaces between the lathes. The second principle involved slide projections, which covered the floor of the set as well as the leafy projection screens.

Figs. 53–55

Svoboda's setting for Weber's opera, *Oberon* (Munich, 1968), was essentially a repeat with elaborations of the setting for *A Midsummer Night's Dream*, as well it might be, of course, since the subject matter of the two works is so similar. Although many more suspended leaf forms were used, as well as other organic forms, the overall goal was the same: the creation of space by the use of colored lighting and projections on stylized natural forms.

Figs. 56–60

A more sophisticated version of the same scenographic principle was evident in the London production of Strauss's *Die Frau Ohne Schatten* (June 1967), but it still aimed primarily at the creation of colored space rather than colored *décor*. "The principle was the same, but its execution was not complicated by shaped screens at odd angles. Instead, I hung them parallel to the proscenium opening. In addition, the forms were more abstract and not merely floral or vegetative." * The forms and colors were abstract embodiments of the forces of good and evil in the opera, as were the two half-moons of stairs

Figure 51. A Midsummer Night's Dream. The side and frontal views of Svoboda's model reveal the basic scenic elements: suspended leaves and a grated floor curving into the rear wall.

Figure 52. Two views of the *Dream* production that suggest the way the projections and suspended forms created a new sense of space.

Figure 53. Svoboda's model for *Oberon.* The numbering on the separate screens suggests the increased complexity of the system in relation to that of *A Midsummer Night's Dream.* Note also the repeated use of leaf-shaped disks in the floor.

Figure 54. Another view of the *Oberon* model, showing the more elaborate scenic units employed in the production.

 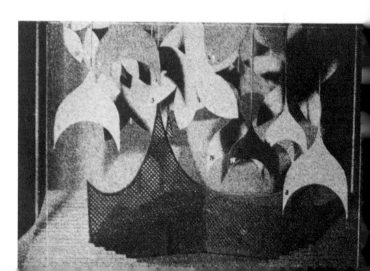

Figure 55. A production photograph of *Oberon* that clearly reveals the huge size of the cutouts. Foto Rudolf Betz, Munich.

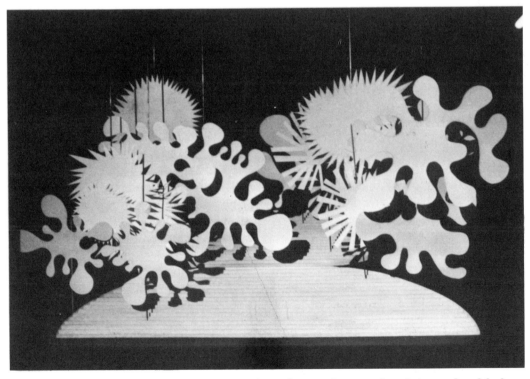

Figures 56–60. Die Frau Ohne Schatten. The series of renderings and models shows the basic elements of varied cutouts, slide-projected abstract forms in color, and two half-moon flights of stairs. Certain scene-changes were effected by the lower stairs lifting to form the roof of a dwelling revealed underneath the stairs.

Figure 57. Svoboda's model with abstract, non-organic cutouts representing the forces of evil.

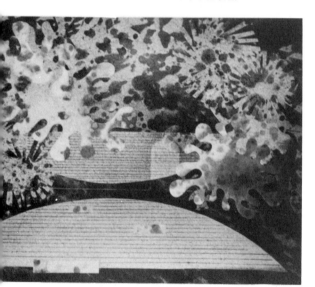

Figures 58 and 59. Two of Svoboda's renderings of the different cutouts with projections on them.

Figure 60. A production photograph of *Die Frau Ohne Schatten.*

that represented the real and poetic worlds that are finally bridged and meet when the protagonist gets back her shadow.

> Previous productions usually approached the opera with banal, conventional fantasy, for instance a road leading to heaven. I wanted to create colored space and a sense of mutability in order to suggest the atmosphere of the work—not theatrical *décor* suggesting would-be fantasy and magic. There were no intermissions or scene-shift pauses, but a constant flow of music and action: a simultaneous kinetic scene with great variability and fine quality slides [18 x 18 cm.] to produce brilliant colors.°

Figs. 61, 62   *Radůz and Mahulena* (Prague, 1970), a Czech folk melodrama with music, provided Svoboda with still another opportunity to work a variation on this basic principle. This time, instead of floral or abstract forms suspended in space, the shaped forms taking the projections were extensions of the stage floor and represented mountain peaks. The triangular, curved, sail-like forms "created a sense of unending natural space (the Tatra mountains) and of varied moods and locales (forests, cliffs). Moreover, the peaks of the triangles could be raised or lowered, thus providing a relatively flatter or more peaked,

Figure 61. Raduz and Mahulena, showing the protagonist chained in a hostile environment.

Figure 62. Raduz and Mahulena, suggesting the notably different effect created by a change in lighting and projection.

Figures 63–69. Pelléas and Mélisande, a further evolution in the creation of colored space or, perhaps better, spatial color. Loosely hung, plastically shaped pieces of wire-scrim material, a cyclorama of special material permitting transmission of colored projection, and abundant use of additive colored lighting, front and rear, were the chief scenic elements. The black-and-white, two-dimensional photographs can only faintly suggest the actual results.

ominous environment. The use of this scenic principle also allowed the many scenes of the opera to follow each other with virtually no interruption." *

According to Svoboda, the second main type of scenography employing projections and color in space could be seen in two productions that were both staged in December 1969: *Pelléas and Mélisande* in London, and *Tannhäuser* in Hamburg. Each production had several distinctive features.

Having progressed as far as *Die Frau Ohne Schatten* with color and light, Svoboda vowed not to do any more with colored settings until he had control of more sophisticated materials and lighting instruments. The opportunity came with the production of *Pelléas and Mélisande,* the chief new technical element being a special cyclorama screen that took not only front and rear projections but also allowed projections as well as additive lighting to pass *through* it to create startling new combinations of color tones and shapes. Another significant difference in technique was found in the shift from deliberately formed, primarily opaque cutouts to loosely hung materials to shape the colored space. Specifically, wire screening was deliberately twisted and squeezed into shapes that didn't need frame supports, thereby creating in space a series of irregular nets that could take projections from the sides as well as from the front or back. Moreover, the raked stage floor had at its upstage end a surface of freely curved, mirrored material that reflected the cyclorama and thereby "pulled" the cyclorama's images and colors to the front; the

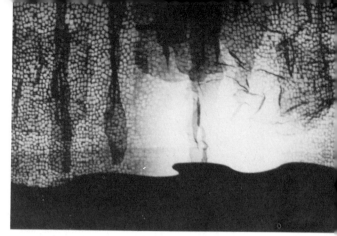

Figure 64. *Pelléas and Mélisande:* the model.
Figures 65–69. *Pelléas and Mélisande:* production photographs.

Figure 70. The forest scenes of *Tannhäuser* were represented by strips suspended in various layers into "pockets" formed by the angles of elevated paths that ran upstage. Projections created the effect of intensely colored autumn foliage.

Figures 71–73. Tannhäuser, illustrating the complex scenographic principle of multiple projections reflected in multiple, specially shaped mirrors.

mirrored surface also eliminated the hard line that usually divides the cyclorama from the floor. Speaking in advance of the production, Svoboda said,

> The goal is the creation of "pseudo" space almost entirely by colored lighting, with virtually no projection of shaped, defined images. Music is again the source of the scenographic design concept, even more than is usual with me; the lighting accompanies and responds to the rhythms of the music. The rear projections and additive lighting through the special cyclorama screen together with the front projections result in a three-dimensional blend of colors and projections and thereby produce a finer quality than was possible in *Frau Ohne Schatten.**

Figs. 70–73   The production of *Tannhäuser* was marked by still further elaboration of the principle of spatial color and projections. Essentially, Svoboda coupled the projection techniques with a varied use of mirrors to multiply and intensify the final effect: a giant collage of images in pseudo-plastic space.

The basis of the scenography was the groundplan. The front peak of the forestage extended partly above the orchestra pit; from this point, the stage extended backward via two sharply angled paths that inclined upward to a height of over six feet at the rear. The angled paths therefore formed several pockets in which actors or dancers could be placed and be "hidden" from the audience. Moreover, the floor of these pockets had a specially treated surface that enabled it to take projections vividly. The mirror technique, mainly employed in the Venusberg sequence, consisted of a series of mirrors of vaguely erotic outline that were suspended at special angles above the paths and their pockets, thus reflecting both the figures in the pockets as well as whatever was projected onto the floor of the pockets. This basic device was multiplied and

Figure 72. Tannhäuser.
Figure 73. A drawing of the scenic arrangement for the Wartburg scene in *Tann-häuser.*

amplified by several others. The front of the mirrors, for example, was covered with scrim and thus could blend a reflected image with a projected one; more-over, the rear surface of each mirror was a projection screen which took rear projections; these in turn were reflected toward the audience by one or more of the other mirrors that happened to hang behind the given mirror. Com-pleting the projection-mirror techniques were direct projections on the raked paths themselves, as well as rear projections on the cyclorama. The resultant collage consisted of the onstage principal performers, a multi-angled projec-tion of colors and images, the multiple reflection of those colors and images, and the reflected images of other performers out of direct view of the audience.

A relatively simpler, non-mirror technique was employed in the forest scenes. Strips of a special scrimlike material, in widths from one to four feet representing trunks of trees, were suspended into the pockets formed by the paths (Figure 69). Projections of color and of leafy patterns were then cast on this vertical "forest" to offset the verticality of the strips when desired. The final effect of setting and projections was not unlike that of parts of the *Pelléas* production.

Similarly, the scenography of the interior Wartburg scene, employing neither mirrors nor projections, resembled that of *Sicilian Vespers* (Figures 48–50) in its use of pure architecture and counter-lighting: architectural units slid into the pockets formed by the paths, and illumination was provided by banks of low-voltage lighting instruments (Figure 73).

In the broad context of Svoboda's recent work, the mirror techniques used in this production resemble those used in *The Insect Comedy* (Figures 126–128) but even more those planned for the Milan production of *The Fiery Angel* (Figures 129–132) because, like the techniques in the latter, they are primarily intended to reflect what is *not* on stage.

A still more complex branch of Svoboda's innovations with light, optics, and projections involves the dramatic *interplay* of cinematic and slide projections with stage action and scenery. As distinct from the projections discussed in the previous section, these not only represent a far greater range of phenomena but are also more inextricably part of the establishment and flow of the dramatic action. As early as 1942 Svoboda had used slide projections in an amateur production, and in 1943 he was already experimenting with a scenario that would combine film projection and live action in a manner directly foreshadowing their union fifteen years later in Laterna Magika: see the sections on *Straying* and *The Eleventh Commandment* (pp. 52–53). Central to Svoboda's use of projection techniques in whatever form are his theatrically oriented concerns with space and synthesis: "We in theatre are constantly aware of space, and we can enhance it by many means, whereas film can only transcribe space. In fact, in theatre we can enhance space by the use of film; that's why theatre is the art of greatest synthesis."[1]

Before proceeding to a closer consideration of several examples in which this type of projection work is crucial—Laterna Magika, Polyekran, and a few of their derivatives—it would be useful to make a brief survey of certain historical predecessors of these more fully evolved forms. Experimentation with static projections that attempt to provide a sense of drama and movement may be traced back as far as the seventeenth century and the crude but vivid use of successive slides devised by the Jesuit, Athanasius Kircher.[2] In the early days of the motion picture, on the other hand, the influence of theatrical scenic conventions on film is evident in the capricious, inventive work of Melies at the turn of the century. Later, a more sophisticated, reciprocal influence between film and stage becomes apparent in the pioneering work of the Russian avant-garde, especially the indirect, aesthetic influence of film on theatre; that is, the gradual adoption by the theatre of those characteristics and techniques that are specifically cinematic, such as the plurality of film: its use of multiple perspectives and a multiplicity, rather than unity, of time, place, and action, as well as the resulting tendency toward montage effects and a rapid, dynamic tempo that captures the rhythms of contemporary life. Such indirect influence is clear in Meyerhold's avant-garde productions in postwar Russia. But the first truly significant adoption of film by theatre is to be found in the work of Ervin Piscator.

1. Svoboda, quoted in "Entretien sur la Lanterne Magique," *Théâtre en Tchecoslovaquie*, pp. 53f.
2. Jan Grossman, "O kombinace divadla a filmu" [The combination of theatre and film], *Laterna Magika*, ed. Jiří Hrbas (Prague, 1968), p. 38. Grossman's article provides a very useful survey of the background and context of work on Laterna Magika.

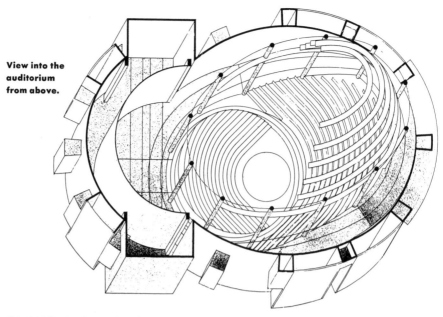

View into the
auditorium
from above.

PLANS AND MODEL OF THE SYNTHETIC
"TOTAL THEATER," 1926

This theater provides a stage in arena form, a proscenium and a back stage, the latter divided in three parts. The 2,000 seats are disposed in the form of an amphitheater. There are no boxes. By turning the big stage platform which is solidary with part of the orchestra, the small proscenium stage is placed in the center of the theater, and the usual set can be replaced by projecting scenery on twelve screens placed between the twelve main columns supporting the structure.

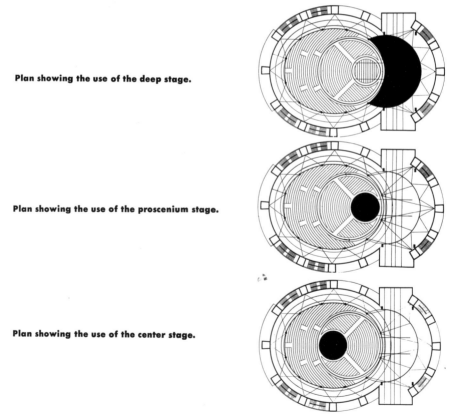

Plan showing the use of the deep stage.

Plan showing the use of the proscenium stage.

Plan showing the use of the center stage.

Figure 74. Gropius's *total-theater* that allowed for front and rear projection on twelve screens surrounding the audience. The project was never realized.

The episodic, fragmented composition of Piscator's dramatic texts, for example, frequently reveals the indirect effect of cinematic montage techniques. Drawing upon his extensive experience with film and slide projection, he also proposed three overlapping uses of these techniques in stage production: the documentary or instructional; the dramatic (when incorporated with the action either as transitional links or simultaneously with stage action); and the editorial, addressing the spectator directly while accompanying the action.[3] His involvement with film even led to a consideration of new forms of theatre structure to accommodate the joint action of film and stage, most notably in the project for a *total-theater,* on which he worked with Walter Gropius. The results of their deliberations were described by Gropius:

Fig. 74

> I accepted his [Piscator's] request to install projection screens and machines everywhere with great interest. . . . I counted on the possibilities of film projection not only on the curved cyclorama of all three depth stages, but I could also project in the entire audience space—on the walls and even the ceiling. For this purpose, projection screens were fastened between twelve supporting columns of the auditorium, on the translucent surfaces of which we could also project from the rear from twelve film projectors. . . . The projections could be supplemented by another cluster of instruments from a projection tower that could project images on the same screens from within the auditorium. . . . In other words, we substituted projection space for the former projection screen.[4]

The projections employed by Piscator, Brecht, and the subsequent American Federal Theatre's Living Newspapers were primarily designed for their instructional, documentary, or alienation purposes, rather than for the creation of atmosphere or emotion, per se. It was precisely a desire to produce an essentially emotive effect, however, that guided the significant projection work of the Czech director, E. F. Burian, during the 1930s. Burian, the most immediate predecessor, if not the inspirer, of Svoboda and his co-artists, staged several productions that made complex and integrated use of film and slide projection in order to create a poetic, lyrical atmosphere, perhaps most notably in his production of Wedekind's *Awakening of Spring* in 1936, designed by Miroslav Kouřil. The production stayed within the limits of a regular proscenium theatre, placing the stage action between two projection screens, the front one a transparent scrim that curved across the entire proscenium opening, the rear one, opaque and smaller, in the upstage left position; a black cyclorama enclosed the stage. A total of four projection machines were used: two slide and one film projector at the rear of the auditorium projected onto the front scrim, and one slide projector offstage right projected onto the screen at upstage left; the film projections were black and white, the

Fig. 75

3. Piscator, *Politische Theatre* (Hamburg, 1963), pp. 169–171.
4. Gropius, quoted by Piscator, p. 128.

Projections and Synthesis 79

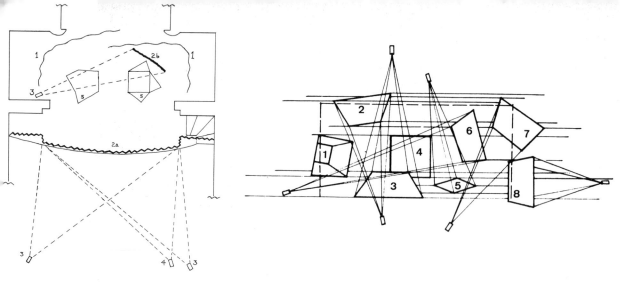

Figure 75. E. F. Burian's Theatergraph. 1—black drape cyclorama; 2a—front projection scrim; 2b—opaque projection screen; 3—slide projectors; 4—film projector; 5—slightly elevated acting platforms. Based on a drawing in *Acta Scaenografica* (March 1966), p. 163.

Figure 76. An early, frontal diagram of Polyekran, which, with minor adaptations, was the basis of the popular exhibit at the Brussels World's Fair of 1958.

slides were in color. A great variety of combinations was available as a result of judiciously blending the intensities of lighting and projections, from the selective lighting of actors in darkened space to the full orchestration of lighted actors against a projected background, as well as seemingly within the projection on the scrim in front of them. Sometimes, figures on stage would be dramatically juxtaposed with the projected image of another character, who was being discussed; or the action on stage would be blacked out and a close-up of one of the characters would be projected onto the front scrim as his speech concluded. The action on stage was complete and coherent in itself, however; the projections were supplemental, and no true interaction occurred between stage and screen. The total system was later named the Theatergraph.

Of the two primary projection systems or forms devised by Svoboda, Laterna Magika and Polyekran, the latter is relatively simpler, and although its evolution is difficult to disentangle from that of Laterna Magika, it was Polyekran that contributed to the final form of Laterna Magika, rather than the other way round, according to both Svoboda and his creative partner Alfred Radok. For these reasons, Polyekran (literally, "multi-screen") will be described first.

Figs. 76–79   Polyekran, as a form, was Svoboda's own contribution to the Brussels World's Fair of 1958; originally, he asked Alfred Radok to prepare a scenario for it and also expected that he would direct it, but as events turned out, Radok's brother, Emil, provided both the scenario and direction.

Figure 77. An early sketch of a proposal for Polyekran.

Polyekran is fundamentally a pure projection form; it is not combined with live acting or scenic elements. Its origin is related to Svoboda's response to the development of various wide-screen film techniques in the 1950s; in contrast to such techniques, all of which attempted to eliminate the impression of a screen and to give the spectator the sensation of being part of the picture, Polyekran deliberately emphasizes the presence of the screen, or, rather, screens. Its principle is a simultaneous and synchronous projection of slides and film on several static screens, during which the images on the individual screens are in dramatic interplay with one another in the creation of a total, organic composition. Svoboda adds:

> Polyekran offers the possibility of free composition, a free shaping and creation on several screens. Real objects and people are projected, but the relationships among them are not realistic, but rather supra-realistic, perhaps surrealistic. Essentially, it's the principle of abstract and pure collage, which is an old and basic technique of theatre. "Op art" is perhaps simply a more recent name for it. In any case, the contrast of varied things on stage is basic to theatre: the objects thereby acquire new relationships and significance, a new and different reality.*

Technically, the elements of the Brussels production consisted of eight screens of various sizes and shapes suspended at different angles from horizontal steel wires in front of a black velvet backdrop. Eight automatic slide projectors and seven film projectors, synchronously controlled by electronic tape, threw images upon these screens. The visual collage was accompanied by stereophonic sound (also carried on the electronic tape), the total ten-minute performance being thematically unified by its depiction of the annual Prague Spring Music Festival.

In form, Polyekran had one somewhat distant forerunner: in 1927, Abel Gance employed a three-screen, triptych-like arrangement for his film *Napoleon.* For the most part, however, Gance did relatively little with complex and

Figure 78. Polyekran employs only projections: simultaneous, multiple images from slides and film.

Figure 79. Polyekran. The photographs illustrate the collage-like interplay of images that defines the form. The variously angled screens were static and essentially in the same plane.

varied juxtaposition of images; moreover, he used the technique for primarily literal, narrative ends.

Polyekran, in slightly revised format, was subsequently presented at the Brno Fair in 1959; more important, its principles formed the scenographic basis for one of Svoboda's major productions, *Their Day*, by Josef Topol, in 1959 (pp. 92–95).

In describing the relation between Polyekran and Laterna Magika, Svoboda said: "In comparison with Polyekran, which is totally a film spectacle and technically a concern of film, Laterna Magika is theatre with living actors, singers, dancers, musicians. . . . On the one hand, we used familiar scenographic techniques such as slide and film projection. New expressive possibilities were added by panoramic film and projection with multi-exposure on several screens at once. A second feature is the use of mobile screens that are joined to the performance of a live actor."[5]

Still another essential element, in addition to mobile screens and live actors, is film that is produced specifically and solely for its use in the given production, rather than film previously made for some other purpose and subsequently incorporated into a separately created stage work.

Svoboda describes the work leading up to Laterna Magika in this way: "Our Laterna Magika arose on the basis of more than fifteen years of joint work with director Alfred Radok. We experimented with some elements of Laterna Magika soon after World War II during productions at the Grand Opera of the Fifth of May, later on the stage of the Tyl theatre, and then especially on the stage of the former theatre of the Czech film organization, where we staged the first production that fully exploited the combination of film and theatre, a dramatization of Šamberk's *Eleventh Commandment*. For this production we even shot a special film"[6] (Figure 24).

Commenting on the essential non-autonomy of each medium, film and living actor, in Laterna Magika, Svoboda added: "The play of the actors cannot exist without the film, and vice-versa—they become one thing. One is not the background for the other; instead, you have a simultaneity, a synthesis and fusion of actors and projection. Moreover, the same actors appear on screen and stage, and interact with each other. The film has a dramatic function."[*]

Laterna Magika becomes, in effect, a new, hybrid medium, the potential force and expressiveness of which are perhaps suggested best in some remarks by Marshall McLuhan made without reference to Laterna Magika, when he writes of "true hybrid energy": "The hybrid or the meeting of two media is a moment of truth and revelation from which new form is born. . . . The moment

5. Svoboda, quoted in "O světelném divadle," *Informační Zprávy* (September 1958), p. 5.
6. Svoboda, "Problémy scény Laterny Magiky," *Laterna Magika*, p. 98.

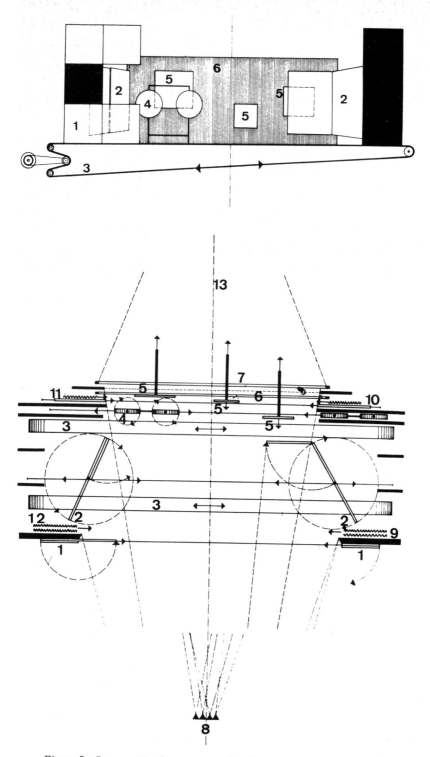

Figure 80. Laterna Magika as presented at the 1958 Brussels World's Fair, ground-plan and frontal view. 1—projection screens hinged along vertical axis; 2—projection screens hinged and rotatable along vertical axis and movable laterally across width of stage; 3—treadmill; 4—circular projection screens rotatable on vertical axis; 5—projection screens movable downstage from the cinemascope screen; 6—cinemascope screen for frontal, wideangle projection, composed of vertical, elastic strips to allow for passage of live actors; 7—cinemascope screen for rear projection; 8—projection booth with three fully synchronized film projectors and one slide projector, these being synchronized with one film projector (behind all the screens) for rear projection; 9—main curtain; 10—two-sided shutter frame curtain; 11—projection screens, laterally movable; 12—scrim curtain; 13—rear projection.

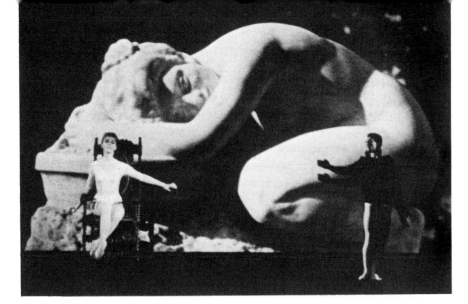

Figure 81. Laterna Magika, a simple juxtaposition employing only the wide screen. Few photos exist of the more complex, multiple image sequences.

of the meeting of media is a moment of freedom and release from the ordinary trance and numbness imposed on them by our senses."[7]

Figs. 80–83 Like Polyekran, Laterna Magika was devised for the Brussels Fair of 1958, where it enjoyed a spectacular success. It consisted of three film and two slide projectors, synchronously controlled, plus a device that enabled deflection of one projection beam to any desired spot, including a moving screen. In a stage space measuring approximately 50′ x 24′ x 20′ were arranged eight types of mobile screens with special, highly directional reflecting surfaces; they could rise, fall, move to the side, fold up, rotate, appear and disappear in precise rhythm with the actors. The stage itself was provided with a moving belt to accommodate the need for virtually instantaneous live action in response to the film. One of the screens, moreover, was equipped with a diaphragmatic framing shutter curtain that could alter both the size and shape of the screen. And the total presentation was enhanced by multi-speaker stereophonic sound.

Jan Grossman, himself a theatre director as well as critic, was involved with the theoretical groundwork of Laterna Magika, and his remarks on the new form elaborate on some of its potentials: "Laterna Magika offered the dramatist, film scenarist, poet, and composer a new language: a language that is more intense, sharply contrasting, and rhythmic; one which can captivatingly project statistics as well as ballet, documents as well as lyric verse, and is therefore capable of absorbing and artistically working over the density and dynamics, the multiplicity and contrariety of the world in which we live."[8]

Alfred Radok, director of Laterna Magika, suggested its special quality

7. Marshall McLuhan, *Understanding Media* (New York, 1966), p. 55.
8. Grossman, p. 76.

in this way: "Above all, Laterna Magika has the capacity of seeing reality from several aspects. Of 'extracting' a situation or individual from the routine context of time and place and apprehending it in some other fashion, perhaps by confronting it with a chronologically distinct event."[9]

That Laterna Magika was not without its special problems, however, became evident even while it was experiencing its greatest success, if not, indeed, even earlier. For example, the complicated integration of film and living performers demanded a formidable amount of time and money. A related though less obvious difficulty was that the filmed portions had to be prepared far in advance of their integration with the live performers, which meant that many artistic decisions had to be made and became binding long before there was any way of knowing how they might work out months later. In other words, the film had to be made in advance, and if the combination with live dancer, for example, didn't work, there simply wasn't time to re-shoot the film to adapt to the dancer. If the dancer, in this situation, couldn't make the necessary adjustment, it meant that the particular sequence probably had to be scrapped. The more profound problem inherent in this situation was that the film virtually enslaved the live performer, whose margin of variability in performance approached zero because the film was a prefabricated element to which the performer must inflexibly adapt. Svoboda put it this way: "It means that Laterna Magika is to a certain extent deprived of that which is beautiful about theatre: that each performance can have a completely different rhythm, that the quality of a performance can be better or worse, that a production can expand its limits."[10] A more material problem was that of appropriate space and facilities both for the preparation of Laterna Magika and for its eventual performance. "All attempts with the medium have occurred in space designed for conventional theatres," said Svoboda, "and such space is not suitable for the medium. It's necessary to build entirely special seating arrangements and stages in order that the principle might be given the widest scope in which to evolve."[11] The nearest approach to a special home for Laterna Magika was a permanent adaptation of a moving picture theatre for Laterna Magika's Prague premiere in May 1959. The resulting structure had some advantages—permanently installed electronic equipment for projections and sound, a specially rigged stage, and optimal sight lines—but it was still restricted by existing and inflexible dimensions.

Again, on a more fundamental level, Laterna Magika never experienced the ultimate test of presenting a work that was written especially for it; that is, a work other than a revue or cabaret entertainment. In its original version,

9. Radok, quoted by Grossman, p. 77.
10. Svoboda, "Problémy scény," p. 103.
11. Svoboda, quoted in "Entretien sur la Lanterne Magique," p. 54.

Figure 82. Laterna Magika. The live performer and the screened images are mutually dependent; they function together simultaneously.

Figure 83. Laterna Magika. Five previously filmed projections of the young man at the piano were synchronized with his stage performance.

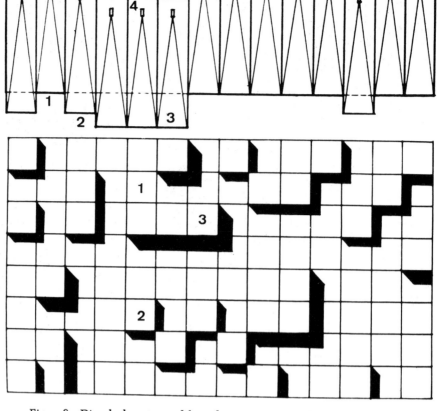

Figure 84. Diapolyekran top and frontal views. 1–3—movable projection cubes with screens for rear projection; 4—two 35mm slide projectors mounted one above the other at the rear of each cube, the multiple projections and movement of all cubes being electronically programmed.

as an entertaining propaganda piece for Czechoslovakia, it was a success. Its original creators had thoughts of eventually using the form for Shakespeare or explorations of challenging contemporary realities, for example the Eichmann case, but managerial and administrative elements viewed Laterna Magika in terms of economics and politics, with the result that its subsequent artistic career was aborted. A version of Martinů's opera, *The Opening of the Wells,* was pre-screened and not allowed to be released, apparently because it offended the residual socialist realist criteria of those who sat in judgment. Svoboda subsequently started work on a version of Offenbach's *The Tales of Hoffmann* but withdrew from the production when he felt that it was being artistically compromised. The original creative team split up for several years, and those who remained or later took over the process have not to this day been able to produce anything more than tourist-level entertainment with it. It is, indeed, a painful and ironic saga, redeemed in part by the opportunity it offered for testing a number of new materials and techniques and for ap-

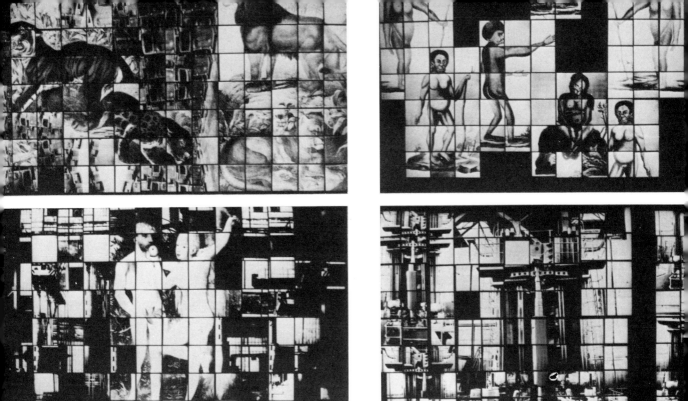

Figure 85. Diapolyekran. The photographs suggest the variety of visual effects obtainable; a distinct rhythm characterized the flow of images.

proaching the realization of a striking new form. Svoboda himself believes that his subsequent work with Radok almost ten years later, on Gorki's *The Last Ones* (1966), partly "rehabilitated the form with new proportions and dimensions and perhaps brought it a few centimeters closer to the goal of a *teatro mundi*." Other productions that employed a basic feature of the form were *Intoleranza* (1965) and *Prometheus* (1968).

Figs. 84, 85 One other noteworthy and recent variant of Svoboda's projection techniques is the Diapolyekran system, which had its first public exposure at the Montreal Expo 67 as a ten-minute feature entitled *The Creation of the World*. It, too, is a multi-screen, multi-projection system reminiscent of Polyekran in its pure film, non-actor features, but in a tighter, shallower, and more stable form. As the illustrations suggest, the projection screens form a wall composed of cubes, 112 in all. Each cube has two automatic 35 mm slide projectors mounted at its rear, capable of flashing five images per second, even though the actual rate was considerably slower; a total of 30,000 slides were used, and the whole operation was computerized. Moreover, each cube was capable of sliding forward or backward approximately twelve inches, thus providing a

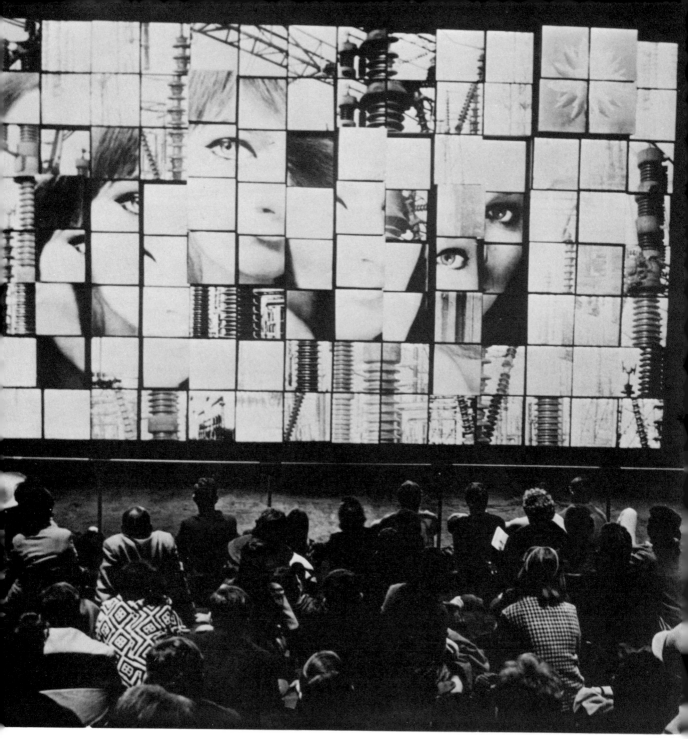

Figure 85. Diapolyekran.

surface in kinetic relief for the projections. The basic technique is of course a collage or montage that allows for a great range of visual effects: the entire wall of cubes may unite to present one total, conventionally coherent picture, or else literally disintegrate that picture in definitively cubistic fashion, or, indeed, present a surrealistic collage of disparate images. And all of this occurs in a dynamic, rhythmic flow ideally suited to projecting *process* as well as startling, abrupt confrontation. The original presentation was an eloquent, sensitive expression of wonder at the miracle and mystery of creation, evolution, and civilization.

Like Polyekran and Laterna Magika, Diapolyekran has also had its theatrically adapted offspring, chiefly *The Suzanna Play* in 1968, *The Journey* in 1969, and *The Soldiers* in 1969.

What is common to all three of these projection techniques is fundamental to virtually all of Svoboda's work: the principle of synthesis, which implies a vivid sense of separate elements imaginatively combined to express new insights into reality. It is a principle that may take a variety of forms, including, for example, cubism, especially as defined in the following remarks by Marshall McLuhan: "Instead of the specialized illusion of the third dimension, cubism sets up an interplay of planes and contradictions or dramatic conflict of patterns, lights, textures. . . . [It] drops the illusion of perspective in favor of instant awareness of the whole. . . . Is it not evident that the moment that sequence yields to the simultaneous, one is in the world of the structure and of configuration?"[12]

The principle of synthesis, especially as seen in Svoboda's projection techniques, also suggests (somewhat ironically) a classic literary antecedent. The words of Samuel Johnson in describing metaphysical wit (an essentially verbal phenomenon) seem singularly appropriate not only to Diapolyekran but, with reservations, to many of Svoboda's other visually oriented works: "Wit . . . may be more rigorously and philosophically considered as a kind of *discordia concors*; a combination of dissimilar images, or discovery of occult resemblances in things apparently unlike. . . . The most heterogeneous ideas are yoked by violence together; nature and art are ransacked for illustrations, comparisons, and allusions; their learning instructs, and their subtlety surprises."[13]

12. McLuhan, p. 13.
13. Johnson, "Abraham Cowley," *Lives of the English Poets.*

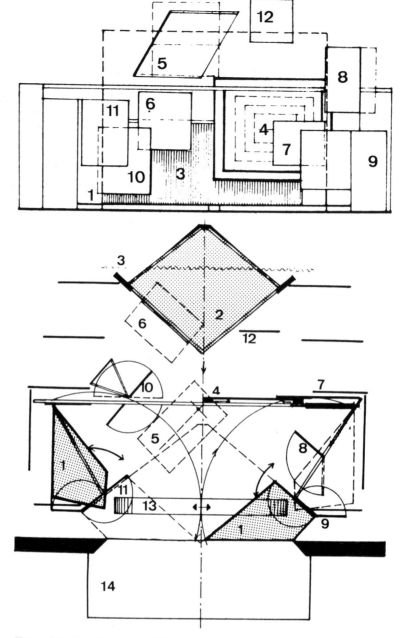

Figure 86. Their Day, groundplan and frontal view. 1, 2—movable platform acting areas; 3—black velvet curtain; 4—projection screen with four-sided shutter curtain; 5, 6—projection screens rotatable along their horizontal axes; 7—projection screen movable laterally across stage; 8, 10, 11—projections screens rotatable along their vertical axes; 9—projection screen foldable along its vertical axis; 12—free hanging projection screen.

"The appearance or disappearance of the screens was accomplished by their being flipped along either their horizontal or vertical axis, or else by their being folded open or shut. One screen (#3) had a four-sided, diaphragmatic shutter curtain that enlarged or diminished the projection surface of the screen. Another screen (#7) could be moved laterally across the stage, parallel to the proscenium arch. . . . The automatic changer cartridges of each projector were operated by an electronic brain installed directly into the projector. The automatic mechanism was controlled by the switchboard for stage lighting. A change in current to the projection bulb was picked up by the electronic brain in the projector and was translated into an impulse that activated the mechanism of the changer. Each cartridge contained ten 13-x-13-cm slides. . . . The stage floor and the special wagons were covered with a 5-mm-thick black felt, which thoroughly dampened the sound of the actors' movements and absorbed the beams of stage light relatively well. Care was taken to maintain a so-called shadow zone between the actors and the projection screens, which enabled us to reduce the level of parasitic light and thereby maintain a necessary quality in the projected pictures. The proper choice of materials in scenic objects and costumes also contributed to this end."—Svoboda, "Nouveaux Éléments," pp. 63–64.

Several Offspring of Polyekran and Laterna Magika

Within a year after the introduction of Laterna Magika and Polyekran at Brussels, Svoboda began to apply their techniques to conventional theatre production. After its initial and partial employment in a production of *The Flying Dutchman* in Prague in February 1959, Polyekran became the basic scenographic principle in the National Theatre's production of a new Czech play, Josef Topol's *Their Day*, in October of the same year. The play, a study of the aspirations and disenchantments of youth in the late 1950s, was notable for its impressionistic, episodic manner.

Figs. 86, 87

In Brussels, the Polyekran system was based on fixed, stable screens; in *Their Day*, Svoboda added a Laterna Magika technique: mobile screens that appear and disappear in rhythmic relation to the movement of other scenic elements: namely, three specially prepared stage wagons that transport such objects as furniture and properties. The basic principle, however, remained that of Polyekran, this time with nine screens distributed in space, in different planes, with two slide projectors covering each screen. Three of the screens, moreover, had film projectors assigned to them; the result was a great flexibility in the choice and blending of pictures at will. Svoboda's subsequent remarks on the production point up its chief characteristics:

> Why Polyekran for this production? The play presents a mosaic of city life, a mosaic that evolves with the action of the play. We deliberately avoided a simultaneous scene because you can't get rid of its scenic elements when you don't want them, no matter how sharp the lighting. Besides, here we wanted changes in the dimensions of space as well as rapid shifts of scene. Because we could project various images at various angles, we could create space and spatial relations at will. My essential point in using projections is the creating of new stage space, not as a substitute for *décor* or establishing a locale. . . . We do not want to do away with traditional painted or plastic scenery and substitute scenery created by lighting—an idea that is not in any case a new one. But we want to attempt composing individual, separate, and distinctive visual perceptions into a new total-image according to a given theme: to convey a given intention by a composition of images, their inter-relationship, their temporal and spatial rhythm.[1]

The projections in conjunction with the use of mobile wagons created a good kinetic scene, one that gave us the possibility of great selection and accent, and also provided for changes and adjustments of elements during rehearsals. An

1. Svoboda, "Nouveaux Éléments," p. 64.

Figure 87. Their Day. The several illustrations reveal a sophistication and adaptation of the Polyekran technique, especially in the mobility of the screens and the combination of live actors and screened images.

important fact about this production was that the original text was essentially a sketch, which was then shaped in the process of rehearsal by author and director, chiefly the latter [Otomar Krejča]. He was mainly responsible for new bits of action, business, and movement that prompted the Polyekran approach. For example, the text may have had people sitting indoors, but the director had them walking outdoors.

For such scenes and others, we projected whole sections of the city the full width of the stage, onto the black velour that enclosed the stage, the images thereby being invisible. But then a traveling screen picks up different parts of the projected image as a character walks along, for instance a row of billboards as he paces back and forth while waiting for someone. The technique is the obverse of film panning; it is as if you were looking through a window at part of your environment, and then the window frame started to move laterally, revealing new surroundings. In another scene, a juxtaposition of projected images creates a special emotive composition. We could use all the screens or only one, not merely to describe a locale, but to establish different relations. The result is a tremendous selectivity that becomes poetic. Interiors, for example, had typical domestic details projected, but in fragmented, distorted perspectives, to eliminate any merely naturalistic illustration. Actors were seen in one perspective, projections frequently in another. Or these scenes could also disappear and suddenly we'd have night, moon, and clouds; that is, the stage would be empty except for two people and one screen. The result is real psycho-plastic space created by transforming the dimensions of space in response to the nature of the scene.

The basis is a confrontation of selected realities: actions, objects, people, plus the accenting of things. For example, an object or projection functions and then disappears, very much like the film techniques of cutting and transitional blending. The method is essentially more persuasive, because more theatrical, than painted sets and usual stage constructions.

Where can the Polyekran technique function uniquely in communicating a point? A good example was the scene of a man being hit by a car. On stage, the man's last steps are accompanied by two film projections behind him. The first slowly pans along the edge of the road; the second, in the opposite direction, is as fast as an auto going full speed. We get the sound of squealing brakes and tires, the rising sound of the engine. The man falls. The auto drives away. The projection becomes that of green grass and primroses.

The larger point is the creation of a total *instrument* to be used on stage like a concert piano. I've been pursuing this goal for twenty years. Krejča says that so far it's an instrument that can only play a child's nursery tunes. But eventually it may be much more. I think, for example, that *The Last Ones* and *The Soldiers* show progress. We must keep on learning to play the instrument.*

Figs. 88, 89 — Two subsequent productions that reveal descent from Polyekran are the operas, *Romeo, Julie a tma* ("Romeo, Juliet, and the Darkness"); performed in Prague (September 1962), and *The Journey*, in Hamburg (March 1969). At the same time, both reveal distinct innovations. The former employed a pipe-rack, scaffolding construction of cubes covered on one or more sides by scrim.

The construction system of cubes was very mobile, the individual cubes being capable of movement in one or more directions. The projections (all black and white slides) on the scrim-covered cubes were mostly single pictures projected on the entire scene; the projected image on several layers of scrim in the various planes of the cubes, especially when the cubes were in motion, achieved

Figure 88. A model of *Romeo, Juliet, and the Darkness,* showing the scrim-covered, mobile cubes.

Figure 89. Romeo, Juliet, and the Darkness. The photograph suggests the striking effect of a full-stage projection on several layers of scrim in widely separate planes.

Figure 90. The Journey, still another descendant of Polyekran, this time with massive cubes and opaque projection surfaces.

Figure 91. The Journey. Front and rear slide and film projections were used; this shot illustrates the strong effect achieved by the projection of negatives.

Figure 92. The Suzanna Play, a wall of immobile screens and rear slide projections.

Figure 93. The Suzanna Play, illustrating another bizarre effect possible with the Diapolyekran method.

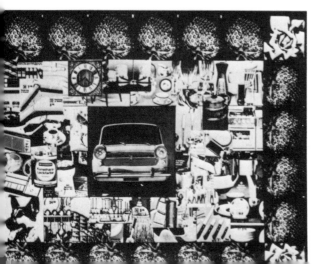 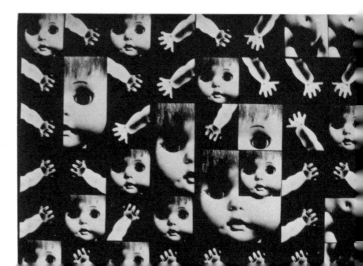

an effect that was more theatrical and poetic than the more precise, compositional method of projections in *The Journey,* for example. I was able to achieve high intensity projections by using four projectors simultaneously, each one projecting a quarter of the total image. The use of cubes in this production was related to the subject matter of the opera, the Nazi occupation of Bohemia; the cubes suggested the life condition of the time, a series of tragedies. For example, in one scene all the cubes except one disappear; the remaining one contains the heroine, alone in a hostile, destructive world.*

Figs. 90, 91   *The Journey* had a smaller number of cubed projection surfaces, all of which were static; they tended to encompass the action in that several were placed at the sides of the stage, perpendicular to the curtain line. At the same time, they presented an essentially solid configuration, as distinct from the framework effect of *Romeo, Juliet, and the Darkness;* this feeling of solidity was enhanced by a complementary production device—the placement of small "rock" orchestras on top of five of the cubes. The theme of the opera—today's civilization confronted with its own emptiness of soul, the grinding down of man by mass media, transport, and industry—lent itself well to the contrapuntal form of the Polyekran system.

The screens in *Their Day,* directly related to those of the original Polyekran, were widely distributed in space; to this characteristic was added mobility. Two very recent, sophisticated variants of Polyekran, *The Suzanna Play* (Frankfurt, November 1968) and *The Soldiers* (Munich, March 1969), reveal the cross-breeding influence of Diapolyekran—a system of rear projections on a multi-screened wall built of relatively small cubes that possess only minimal, back-and-forth mobility. The symmetry and relatively dense concentration of the cube-screens allowed for a special forcefulness of patterned visual imagery.

Figs. 92, 93   *The Suzanna Play* production was a direct descendant of Diapolyekran: forty-eight cubes were symmetrically and linearly arranged in an eight-by-six pattern; eighty slides were devoted to each screen. "The grotesque effects attainable by projecting realities in startling relational patterns,"* as Svoboda expressed it, were particularly suitable to this satiric, capricious comedy of the absurd, dealing with the life cycle of a female product of our civilization. An unusual feature of the projection system was its means of control, with the cueing of the projections composed as a musical score and then controlled electronically from a piano keyboard.

Figs. 94–98   Zimmermann's opera *The Soldiers* is the latest product in the evolution of the Polyekran and Diapolyekran forms; it follows the latter more closely in that its screens are, with one dramatic exception, immobile and rather tightly clustered together in parallel planes. They depart from the Diapolyekran model, however, in being far fewer (thirteen), much larger (as much as 18′

Figure 94. The Soldiers, showing virtually all of the screens being used, and a juxtaposition of photographs and Goya drawings depicting wars in several different periods.

x 12'), and in several planes. Another distinctive feature is the placement of two box-like spaces in the midst of the screens, spaces which may be used as interior acting areas or curtained off to form two screens. Rear projection is employed on all the screens, and the two acting areas just mentioned have front projections as well. Black and white slides form the basis of projection, with film projection being available for three of the screens.

A striking example of the evolutionary process in Svoboda's creative work with a given form is the kinetic variant of the Diapolyekran principle employed at the climax of the opera: the total cluster of screens literally disintegrates, the screens separating from one another and moving off stage. As they sink below stage level, rise up out of sight, or move off laterally, a huge, futuristic "war machine" grinds forward toward the footlights, accompanied by a pulsating, increasingly blinding light and ear-shattering dissonant music.

> With the help of improved instruments and materials, and with new placement and composition of the screens, I was able to create a concentrated, massive visual impact, a collage of military life from Rome to the Franco-Prussian War in confrontation with World War II and Vietnam. Especially effective was the juxtaposition of Goya's etchings with photographs depicting intolerance and martyrdom today. The sheer size of the stage and auditorium [the Munich

Figure 95. The Soldiers. The two acting spaces within the screens are revealed, the back wall of each receiving rear projection. The photograph suggests as well the interesting effects derived from different proportions among the screened images and between the images and the live actors, seen here in silhouette in the acting spaces.

Figure 96. The Soldiers. Both acting spaces are in use as well as the stage floor in front of the screens.

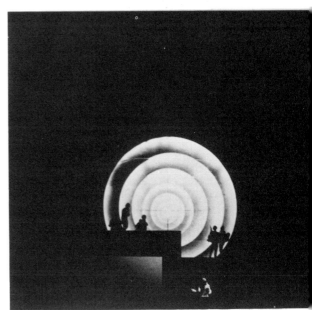

Figure 97. The Soldiers. A fine example of the sheer impact of a stark repetition of the same image on all the screens.

Figure 98. The Soldiers. The climax and ending of the opera, when all the screens are withdrawn, and a futuristic war-machine grinds toward the audience accompanied by light of blinding intensity.

Several Offspring of Polyekran and Laterna Magika 99

Figure 99. *The Last Ones.* The basic scenic elements of production, including a deliberately crumpled projection screen and an incongruously placed upper alcove for small orchestra.

Figure 100. *The Last Ones,* showing a full-screen projection functioning as indirect comment on the stage action. The curtain outlining the screened-off alcove is deliberately retained.

Staatsoper] was another factor: aiming at psycho-plastic space, I designed everything with the proportions of the theatre in mind.*

What is especially interesting is that Svoboda does not feel that he has yet found the right dramaturgic material for the Diapolyekran system:

> The form has yet to be employed with a congenial artistic-poetic text, at least not in the same sense that other forms or devices reached full realization, for example the use of mirrors in *The Insect Comedy,* or Laterna Magika in *The Last Ones. The Soldiers* comes closer to it than *Suzanna,* but the ideal complement would be an opera by Luigi Nonno called *Fabrika,* written specifically with this form in mind. But it has yet to find a producer. It is a work that places its chorus in the orchestra pit, and replaces the conventional orchestra with taped electronic, concrete music. Moreover, Nonno is a composer who, like Orff, is willing to make certain adaptations in having his work produced with new forms.*

Figs. 99–103 A production that particularly satisfied Svoboda during recent years was Gorki's *The Last Ones,* done by Prague's National Theatre in September 1966 under the direction of Alfred Radok. It was the first work they did together after a lapse of several years, and it featured, in Svoboda's words, "a revision, a refinement of Laterna Magika,"* the idea of which had interested him more than twenty years previously, and on which he had worked with Radok as early as 1950, in *The Eleventh Commandment.*

The Last Ones indicts a whole era and regime in depicting a family dominated by a tyrannical, insecure career officer. The deterioration of values, the shabbiness of life, the compromises and stupidities, the cruelties inflicted and

Figure 101. The Last Ones. Another example of the varied emotive effects derived from the juxtaposition of related but strongly contrasting elements.

Figure 102. The Last Ones. The photograph illustrates the composition in depth characteristic of the production: three separate though metaphorically related actions (the last one screened), with a fourth ambivalently related to them, detached from the action yet clearly responsive to it.

endured, all of these social deformations are mirrored, with frequent irony, in the family's material and spiritual bankruptcy. The inherent duality of the subject, the family and its larger social frame, blended superbly with the Laterna Magika form, the very nature of which is rooted in a juxtaposition and interplay of elements: the dramatic integration or counterpoint of screened image and live actor, of the same character on film and on stage, and the powerful, implicitly ironic comment of the one on the other.

Radok's comments provide a useful perspective:

> The production leaned on Gorki as a psychologist and philosopher. But because Gorki as a dramatist placed his characters in a realistic room missing only one wall, we had to bring the characters onto the stage. Some means employed by the production are illogical on the plane of life-like probability. But it's possible to understand them on an emotional level. Frequently a dual, antithetical action will operate on several levels. For example, on stage and on film, in the text and in the music that accompanies the text. . . . What results is a collage of numerous realities: a white wall, a balustrade with chandelier and a small theatrical curtain, a heavy wooden door supported by columns, a cracked piano, and an empty, raked stage platform. On it, ceremonially, the actors place the objects of life: a table, bed, screen, wheelchair. Invisible doors appear or disappear . . . they emphasize the dynamics of entrances and exits.[2]

Svoboda's observations on the production suggest its significance for him:

2. Radok, "Zrod Laterny Magiky a její inscenační principy" [The birth of Laterna Magika and its principles of production], *Laterna Magika*, pp. 24, 27.

Figure 103. The Last Ones, providing the most direct example of the evolution of the
Laterna Magika principle: the same actor on screen as on stage; the action of the screened
image directly related to that of the live performer. As this photograph suggests, however,
the principle was treated with much greater subtlety and complexity in *The Last Ones*
than in *Laterna Magika.*

In effect, we rehabilitated the Laterna Magika principle after its discreditation by commercial interests; this production expressed our credo, an honest application of Laterna Magika, with certain changes and the addition of new techniques. Originally, Laterna Magika operated with a lateral format of images and stage action, but in *The Last Ones* we changed this to a depth principle in order to create a cumulative effect, to increase the impact rather than disperse it, to intensify. We stacked things, people, scenes behind each other; for example, action around the wheelchair downstage, above that a girl in a tub being stroked by twigs, "in front" of her a boy being flogged on the screen; then, suddenly, a drape covering part of the screen opens and we see a small, live orchestra playing a waltz, with pomp—an image of the regime. A space collage using a triptych principle, truly a dramatic poem—what I want to do. A clear spatial aesthetic is formed by the contrast of stage action, flat projection, and live orchestra behind the screen on which the images are projected. It's all structured like music, and a law is present. Break it and a new one is set up. This is what attracts me—leitmotifs and repetitions, then sudden contrast; plus tempo indications. Themes disappear only to crop up again later. Radok is especially good at this. Why the crumpled projection screen? I wanted to prove that you *can* project on a relief surface with a depth of more than 15 cm and create the effect of a smooth surface; and then, too, the surface at other times suggests the deteriorated conditions depicted by the play.*

Other variations of the Laterna Magika principle have included the Boston production of Luigi Nonno's opera, *Intoleranza* (February 1965), and the Munich production of Carl Orff's opera, *Prometheus* (August 1968); both productions employed closed-circuit, live television projection and videotape recording, thus solving one of the inherent problems of Laterna Magika by freeing the actors from slavery to a previously made, inflexible film. Svoboda's description of the *Intoleranza* production is thorough:

Figs. 104–106

> Instead of film I used television techniques in such a way as to project a TV image onto many screens placed on the stage, up to a size of 16' x 12'. We were able to transmit parallel actions that were performed in adjoining studios, in fact in studios as far as three miles from the stage. All of these studios were joined with each other by audio and visual monitors, so that the actors could see the conductor in relation to themselves, the actors in the studio could see what was being played on stage, and on the contrary the actors on stage could see what was played in the studios. In this way, the conductor was absolute master of the rhythm of the performance. Moreover, television provides the possibility of transmitting actual scenes onto the stage screen, for instance a street in Paris, or wherever else on earth; and it's possible to preserve this picture or image on tape, which is what we did. In fact, we used a thirty-second delay to project onto the stage an action that had already taken place there; in other words, I confronted the actor with a recorded picture of his former action, and so on. It's also possible to transmit an actual picture of the audience

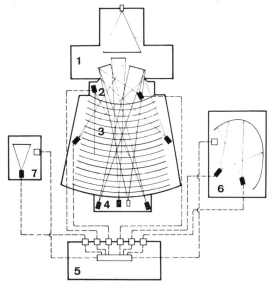

Figure 104. *Intoleranza* (Boston), groundplan. 1—stage with projection screens for television projection (live and on videotape) and rear projection by film; 2—orchestra pit; 3—auditorium; 4—projection booth; 5—monitoring and control center; 6—studio used for chorus scenes; 7—studio for special effects.

Figure 105. *Intoleranza* (Boston), a combination of multiple projections (front and rear) and multiple screens. Here we see a projected live negative image of the performer herself.

Figure 106. *Intoleranza* (Boston). A live chorus on stage, their live video image projected above them, and their imminent "drowning" indicated by rising beams of light.

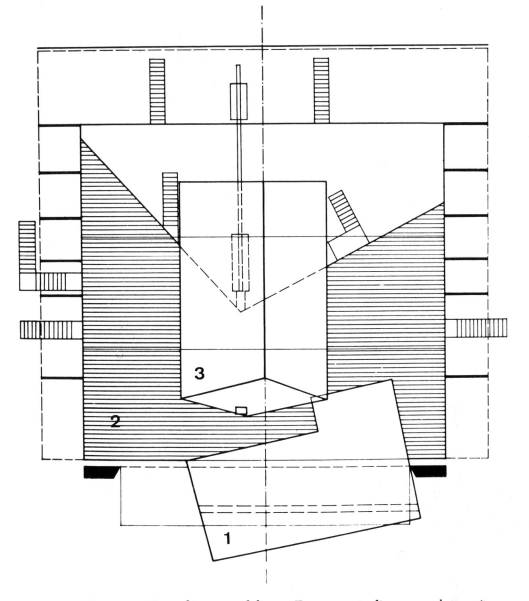

Figure 107. Prometheus, groundplan. 1—Forestage extending over orchestra pit; 2—stairs; 3—movable shaft—Prometheus is bound to its front surface; the metallic, trapezoidal surface also functions as a projection surface for live television projection.

onto the stage. In all such cases you can also project a negative image, which proved very effective in visual comments on racial prejudice. The director is able to work with live images from the very first rehearsal. The pictures projected onto the screens can be filmed with exactness and set down on tape. We can try out parallel actions precisely, those that are going on in appropriate settings on adjoining stages or in adjacent rehearsal rooms.*

Intoleranza also made use of the low-voltage curtains or walls of light, but in a new and special manner. A prime example was the use of such light to "drown" a mass of people on stage; in the wings at each side of the stage, a strip of low-voltage units was placed in a horizontal position, aiming across at the other side of the stage, in the identical plane as its mate. Then, with the crowd on stage, the two strips were slowly raised and created the effect of a sheet of water slowly rising, above the knees, the waist, and so on.

Figs. 107–111   *Intoleranza* was essentially a production based on Laterna Magika principles, but employing television instead of film techniques. *Prometheus*, relying much less on projections, also made more economical and concentrated use of live television, and used the intense, low-voltage lighting principle in still another dramatic fashion, as Svoboda's description makes clear:

> The chief problem in any production of *Prometheus* is that the protagonist is immobilized for two and a half hours while discussion dominates action. There is real danger of boredom, even when, as in this case, fine music is involved; the problem is how to express it. Orff's music conveyed an image of metal to me, resonant metal planes and angles. I recalled the principle of steps that I used in *Oedipus*—steps being a "key" for me with Greek drama—and I adapted it here, covering the steps with a metallic surface. But I added a notch in the top of the stairs, and a diamond-shaped, piston-like shaft, some fifty feet long, that rested in the notch, the front surface of the shaft presenting a rock-like metal surface to which Prometheus is nailed. The shaft slides out slowly to a height of some twenty-five feet above the orchestra pit; the chorus is on the stairs, about fifteen feet below Prometheus. I used projections on the stairs and the rock, the surface of which was rusted, oxidized, textured. But the main device was the use of live television to project an enlarged image of Prometheus' face onto the very surface of the rock to which he was nailed; in other words, we saw Prometheus "in" the image of his face, thereby providing tremendous emphasis to his torment. We used the technique at special moments only, for maximum impact. The ending, during which I used dozens of low-voltage units, had its own special effectiveness. I had the entire frame of the proscenium lined with low-voltage units aimed at the rock and Prometheus. During the ending of the opera, the intensity of these units was gradually increased at the same time that the rock was gradually being withdrawn. The intensity of the special lights increased to a painful, blinding glare in which the TV image faded and the rock began to function as a mirror. The audience was blinded for nearly a full minute; in the meantime the whole setting—the rock and the stairs—disappeared, leaving only blank space. Prometheus was consumed in a fire of light. *

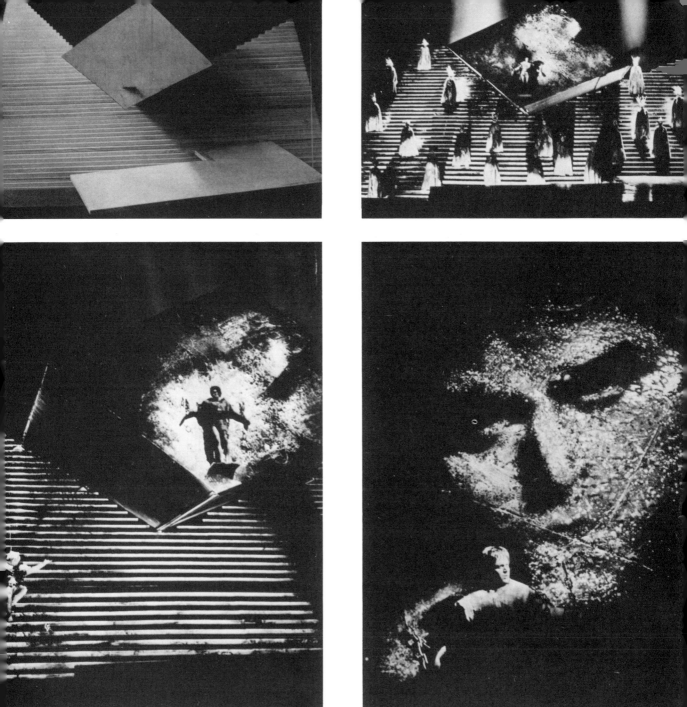

Figure 108. Prometheus, a frontal view of Svoboda's model.
Figures 109–111. Prometheus, showing three views of the actual production, the last suggesting the powerful effect of projecting a simultaneous, enlarged live video image of the actor directly next to the live actor. Note also the effect of the textured metallic surface on which the image is presented. Foto Rudolf Betz, Munich.

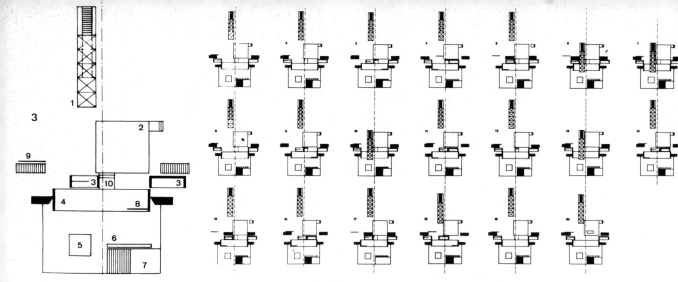

Figure 112. Romeo and Juliet, groundplan for one of the twenty basic settings. 1—movable arcade that also functioned as a balcony; 2—acting platform elevatable to a height of approximately eight feet; 3—movable, heavy framed flats, one with a detachable window piece; 4—special proscenium frame; 5—trapdoor, in two sections, separately elevatable (used for table, bed, fountain, and catafalque); 6—wall unit, elevatable from floor level to a height of approximately nine feet; 7—stairs to orchestra pit; 8—detachable flat; 9, 10—movable staircase units.

Figure 113. Romeo and Juliet, groundplan showing the twenty different scene settings.

Kinetics, Lighting, and Mirrors

Figs. 112–121

Romeo and Juliet, as presented by the National Theatre in Prague (October 1963), under the direction of Otomar Krejča, was a milestone production in which Svoboda fused his principle of dynamism with his profound sense of architecture. The resultant scenography, based on kinetic architecture, provided a definitive example of the creation of one kind of psycho-plastic space, stage space that is fluidly responsive to the emotive demands of the action.

The setting extended over the orchestra pit and consisted of a remarkably homogeneous, intricately balanced group of architectural components—platforms, frames, walls, plinths, stairs—representing various objects and locales as well as purely architectural supplements. Essentially neutral in form, except for a few pieces (such as the scenic *pièce de résistance,* a graceful Renaissance arcade that seemingly floated along an upstage-downstage axis[1] at a height of ten or twelve feet above stage level), the architectural elements were covered with a rough canvas that in turn was covered with a thin burlap, the final suggestive effect being that of the structural façade of a Renaissance palace. The separate elements could form a seemingly infinite number of static spatial compositions or else go into an orchestrated series of movements: rising, sinking, advancing, retreating, or moving laterally.

1. Actually, the arcade was supported by a narrow black plinth that slanted obliquely toward the rear, thereby being virtually invisible from the audience.

Figure 114. Svoboda's model for the Prague *Romeo and Juliet,* showing one of its many possible configurations.

Several aspects of the scenography were especially noteworthy. For example, the production amply vindicated Svoboda's policy of small, component machinery for the stage, readily assemblable for a specific production. Consisting of small motors, pulleys, belts, jacks, and springs, the machinery not only made the sheer variety of movement possible but also cut the total time for scene changes down to four and a half minutes, rather than the customary three-quarters of an hour. Equally impressive was the dramatic quality of the movement, especially in its dramatic counterpoint to the movement of the actors during scene changes, which became, in Svoboda's words, "dramatic

Figures 115–120. Romeo and Juliet. The series of photographs reveals some of the variety of configurations of the architectural elements made possible by movement and lighting.

caesuras in the action, a new type of 'curtain' without curtains, like a cinematic cross-fade, reinforced by carefully plotted, expressive lighting." *

Finally, the mobile architectural scenography created a paradoxical impression of lyric grace and menace. The delicate, airy arcade suspended in space, offset by the seemingly irresistible meshing of solid structures, was a remarkably suggestive embodiment of the antagonistic forces within the play.

Svoboda's dominant memory of this complex scenographic achievement is characteristically non-technical. When asked about the production, he talked far more readily about the humanistic, Renaissance proportions of the architectural elements in relation to the characters and the production's tremendous success with youth than he did about the technical wonders of the performance. "It filled the theatre for five seasons with young audiences; it showed youth that feelings and sensitivity exist and are worth sacrifice." *

Figs. 122–125 The production of a new Czech play by Milan Kundera, *Majitelé Klíčů* ("Owners of the Keys"), in April 1962, was noteworthy for the complex, highly expressive use of both stage kinetics and lighting, the latter combining special use of low-voltage instruments with principles of reflection.

Figure 121. Svoboda's model for the *Romeo and Juliet* production in Cologne in May 1969, an interesting variation of the scenography in the earlier Prague production.

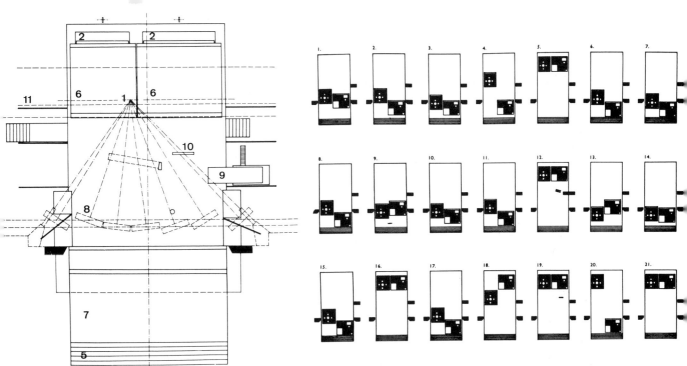

Figure 122. Owners of the Keys, groundplan. 1—suspended mirror; 2—rear walls of wagon stages framed by four-sided shutter curtains; 5—stairs leading off forestage; 6—wagon stages; 7—forestage; 8—strips of high intensity lighting units aimed at mirror; 9—catapult unit used during vision scenes; 10—gallows unit used during vision scenes (see figure 124); 11—black curtain drawn in front of wagon stages during vision scenes.

Figure 123. Owners of the Keys, groundplans of the twenty-one settings.

The play itself, a domestic drama taking place during the Nazi occupation, concerns a young man, formerly an underground resistance worker, who withdrew from his dangerous activity upon getting married and now lives with his wife's parents, who epitomize a narrow-minded cautiousness and need for security. One day, the protagonist is approached by his former comrades for help on a dangerous mission. The dramatic action focuses on his inner struggle in choosing between his very real but limited duty to his domestic circle and the broader appeal of the cause for which his whole nation is fighting. The basic action involves a simultaneous scene: action alternates and frequently overlaps between two rooms occupied by the younger and older couple, respectively. In addition to this *real* action, however, the drama contains a number of *visions:* embodiments of the inner workings of the protagonist's mind during the critical moments of the play. The greatest challenge for the staging was how to combine the two levels of action and their respective scenographic demands. The director, Otomar Krejča, defined the critical problem:

Figure 124. Owners of the Keys, showing simultaneous action on the wagon stages.

...every new dramatic work demands its own distinctive treatment of space.... What sort of space will contain the visions? "George stands in the middle of empty space." How does one create emptiness—"unfathomable, barren space"— in an area of a few square meters? And so I asked Josef Svoboda for "absolute" space ... on the one hand it had to be extremely variable, on the other always— somehow—definable. . . . . We became especially attracted to the idea of a hollow pyramid. Its base, formed by the portal of the stage, would face the audience, and its peak would be at some infinite point. But in the Tyl theatre the "infinite" is a few meters from the curtain line. And what would the hollow pyramid be made of? . . . And so we arrived at a pyramid that, according to need, would or wouldn't exist. It would be made of *light* . . . like living matter, which can be born before our eyes . . . in which everything will seem more real than reality.[2]

Svoboda's relatively detailed description of his scenographic contribution provides a typical example of the practical considerations in his creative process:

The rapid alternation of action in two separate interiors, the interspersion of actual action by the imaginary action of the visions, in short the total dramatic structure of the play was scenically solvable in a positive fashion only kinetic- ally—that is, by means of a scenography tightly bound up with the develop- ment of the dramatic action. In our production, for example, the simultaneous

2. Krejča, "Režie" [Direction], *Milan Kundera: Majitelé Klíčů,* ed. Vladimír Jindra (Prague, 1963), pp. 20–21.

Figure 125. Owners of the Keys, one of the visions. The sense of empty space is created by the pyramid of light reflected from the mirror at its apex.

scene established by the text had the added possibility of appropriate change in response to the actions and words of the play, thanks to the movement of the setting's individual parts.

The basis of the setting became two interiors set next to each other. . . . If our setting was to be tied to the character of the action and to respond to its details and incidents, then it became necessary to create an impression of the appearance and disappearance of the actual interiors in the abstract space of a vision. The spectator was to perceive the withdrawal and approach of both interiors, their fading away, a sense of their diminution and enlargement, not only for the sake of the vision interludes but primarily for the sake of the interrelation of the action transpiring on both acting platforms; for example, the relative emphasis of one interior over the other in given scenes. The chosen movement along an axis perpendicular to the viewer created, during the interspersed visions, a true sense of transference from drama to reality. Thus we technically achieved a fluid shift between individual scenes and drama visions, as well as a sense of the fluid relationships and situations within the scenes of the actual world.

The transition to the visions is accomplished by the mere withdrawal of the wagons behind a black curtain in the background. What is left is a bare, black space with steps connected to the orchestra pit, and given form only by lighting and a few functional details demanded by the action. The return move-

Figures 126–128. The Insect Comedy. The slanted mirrors at the rear of the stage reflect multiple images of the actors and the decorated floor of the rotating turntable.

ment of the wagons to the acting space of the stage creates a true impression of being awakened to reality and strengthens the effect of the drama.[3]

The interiors arranged on both wagons are indicated by only a single white wall each, on which are placed characteristic details: the father-in-law's collection of clocks, and the architectural photographs and charts above the young protagonist's desk. A four-sided black diaphragmatic shutter-curtain is stretched along the edges of each wall; it opens and closes from the center to the edges and vice-versa. The movement of the shutter-curtain is synchronized with the movement of the wagons; during their forward movement it automatically opens, and during their reverse movement it closes again, thereby creating the illusion of the diminution and enlargement of the interiors. In connection with the backward movement, the illusion of a withdrawal to infinity is strengthened: a sense of becoming lost in a dream space.

A frame of low-voltage lighting units is installed in the plane of the proscenium opening. Lighting sources that cast a thin cylinder or "thread" of light

3. Svoboda's added technical details include the following: "The area of the stage . . . is covered in black: the floor by black, light-absorbing felt, the rest by ordinary black velour. Tubular tracks are laid on the floor of the stage; both wagons move along these tracks on rubber wheels. . . . Both wagons, which move along a ten-degree incline and are levelled by the construction of their floors, are hauled by a steel cable fastened across a beam to a normal line in the fly system and counterweighted to a zero point. They move very easily along the tracks with only a slight pull, they are soundless, and they are controllable with a precision tolerance of five centimeters." Svoboda, "Scéna," *Milan Kundera: Majitelé Klíčů,* p. 26.

are set in strips of ten each. Six of these strips lie along the top lighting bridge and four are set on each side of the proscenium opening. At the beginning of the play, the top strips create a curtain of light: the threads of light are aimed perpendicularly downward and are reflected back at the same angle by mirrors set in a grating that lies in the stage floor in the plane of the proscenium opening. The curtain of light separates the action proper from its pictorial introduction, a certain foreshadowing of the dramatist's surgical method: within the utterly black space of the stage, a single thread of light is reflected at an angle from a square mirror (80 x 80 cm) hung from the flies.[4]

As soon as both wagons retreat behind the curtain (placed at a depth of forty feet from the proscenium opening) at the rear of the stage, the space to be used for all four visions appears. It is an abstract space created by a cluster of light beams from the low-voltage sources in the proscenium frame that are aimed at the mirror, which reflects the beams back at the same angle to the proscenium frame. The result is the impenetrably bordered, sharply defined, unreal space of a pyramid created by light.

The setting attempted, by kinetic means, to intensify the dramatic binding of the scenes and dialogue. In conjunction with the thorough and precise directorial composition of the actors' movements, it succeeded in creating a fully unified stage picture.[5]

Figs. 126–128 Svoboda has designed two productions of the modern Czech classic, *The Insect Comedy*, by the Čapek brothers; the first production, in 1946, was his premiere in the National Theatre. The second production, which concerns us here, occurred almost twenty years later (January 1965), again in the National Theatre; as a matter of fact, it is still in the active repertoire of the company and has toured through most of Europe. The play, an episodic, satiric parable of mankind viewed in the image of an insect world, is an open invitation to a designer's creative fantasy. Svoboda was especially pleased with his scenography for the production: "I would always like to approach a work as deeply as I succeeded in doing here, achieving this level of integration."* In brief, the scenography represented a fusion of a basic image or concept of the play with expressive scenic principles, in this case special application of two of Svoboda's recurrent but variable techniques: kinetics and mirrors (evident

4. A contemporary review of the production described this effect vividly: "The performance is preceded by a graphic image: a needle of light is projected against a square mirror hung high above a dark, curtainless stage. The reflection slices across the black space diagonally in a single thin ray that suggests surgery or an X-ray. It is unmercifully white, cruelly sharp and searching." Sergei Machonin, clipping from *Literární Noviny* (May 1962).

5. Additional details: "The scenic objects necessary for the visions emerge from the stage floor, in which they have been set (a ladder, post, gallows). At one point a catapult rides in from the wings, to be used for the scene of the young wife's burning. The details are supplemented by pin-point lighting and sharp counter-lighting on the forestage and orchestra ascent stairs." Svoboda, "Scéna," pp. 25–26.

in *Owners of the Keys* and other plays, but here used in a distinctively different manner).

When the play was considered for part of the repertoire again, years after I
had first designed it, I simply wasn't able to respond to it, to come up with
a design that satisfied me. So I reluctantly turned it down and it was dropped
from the repertoire plans. Later, once I was free of the responsibility of having
to design it, I was playing with a mirror, and suddenly I saw it all clearly—
how to reveal the sheer multitudinousness of man, the sheer numbers that
make one question the difference between insects and people. For instance, the
disturbing or depressing feeling you sometimes get at a busy railway terminal
or airport—how to project this on stage?

The final set embodied the answer: two large mirrors (about 25′ x 25′) set
at special angles at the rear of a turntable. No flats or scenic decor were used,
but the floor of the rotating turntable became a positive motif when covered
with varicolored carpets, a different one for each scene. Only the floor was lit:
we thereby gained light via reflection and also avoided the technical problems
of directly lighting the mirrors. In fact, we created space by means of the overhead view provided by the mirrors: two mirror surfaces in themselves would
multiply the image reflected, but their honeycombed segmentation is what
chiefly created the effect of space and multiplicity here. The six-sided shape
of the segments had the added advantage of being a biological key sign·and
being easy to assemble. The sheer size of the mirrors was made feasible by a
new process that enabled us to put a silver covering on lightweight plastic.

It was an example of scenography precisely expressing the play, of a design
hitting the nail on the head one hundred per cent; there were no holes in the
conception or execution. It was also an example of the technical being absolutely in the service of the total production, and not obtrusive. It wins the spectator over; not until later does he wonder how it was done. A good example of

refinement was the use of ultra-violet light in the moth scene: the moths were represented by gauzy handkerchiefs handled by "invisibly" costumed actors and specially treated to pick up the ultra-violet light.

Today, using newer techniques, we could do even more—especially with flexible, pneumatic mirrors that could alternately shrink and enlarge each image and increase the number of objects mirrored.[*]

Figs. 129–132 The pneumatic mirrors of which Svoboda spoke in relation to *The Insect Comedy* have in fact now become available, and he planned to use them in a production of Prokofiev's *The Fiery Angel,* scheduled for La Scala in the 1970–71 season, but eventually cancelled. Svoboda believes that the deliberate distortions that the mirrors can introduce would be particularly appropriate to the irrational, nightmarish, visionary aspects of the opera.

Svoboda's plans called for scenography similar to that of *The Insect Comedy* but more sophisticated: a large oval mirror suspended at 45° over a turntable that can be lowered almost nine feet below stage level. The mirror would consist of six-sided segments, each of which would be capable of changing from concave to convex by remotely controlled changes in air pressure behind their flexible surface. The mirrors would reflect whatever was on the turntable as well as part of the rotatable ring that encircles the turntable at stage level. Svoboda planned to have up to a dozen layers of variously designed carpets on the turntable; peeling off the successive layers would provide variations in the reflected images and indicate shifts of scene. Alternatively, the rotating turntable with black velour covering and a prone actor making appropriate movements on it was intended to provide a hallucinatory illusion of a flying angel. This latter example is reminiscent of the *Tännhauser* production (pp. 75–76), in which Svoboda also used mirrors to reflect action and projection not otherwise visible on stage.

Indeed, projections would also have been used in this production as they were in *Tännhauser.* Svoboda planned to project images on the turntable and also on the mirror itself, the surface of which was to be covered with scrim for this purpose. Frontal projections on the whole set were to be used when scenic elements were brought on stage from behind the mirror by the rotating ring; the use of a full frontal projection at such times was intended to make the scene shifts less naked, more poetic.

With reference to his total *œuvre,* the scenography of *The Fiery Angel* marked yet another noteworthy synthesis on expressive techniques by Svoboda, those of kinetics, mirrors, and projections.

Figure 129. A model of *The Fiery Angel,* showing the turntable at very nearly stage level.

Figure 130. The turntable is lowered out of sight, but its image is still reflected to the audience by the mirror.

Figure 131. This photograph of the model suggests how additional scenic elements, such as the ladder, may be employed as well as some of the potentially surrealistic effects that should be available when the distorting surfaces of the mirrors have suitably bizarre images to reflect.

Figure 132. The rotatable ring extends behind the mirror. Scenic units, such as those illustrated here in the model, may be placed on the ring behind the mirror and wheeled to the front of the stage.

Figs. 133–138

The production of John Osborne's *The Entertainer* by the National Theatre in Prague (December 1957) was a major success and a good example of the cooperative artistic efforts of Svoboda and Alfred Radok, both of whom instinctively respond to the metaphoric and theatrical potentials of a script. Osborne's study of a disenchanted, aging music hall performer confronted with the futility of his existence, played out in his domestic circle and on stage, provided various opportunities for the stage poetry that attracts both Radok and Svoboda.

Svoboda's basic device was a series of lateral curtains that functioned in several ways; for example, they offset the cubic shape of the stage by their vertical folds and they facilitated fluid transitions between scenes. His own remarks take up other levels of significance:

> I used a setting based on curtains because the play dealt with an entertainer who is leaving the theatre. There is a certain pathos in curtains, per se, but the point here was the *schluss*, a period, the end of a life. So different kinds of colored curtains were run on trolley wires (which represent another world, the larger one, civilization). Suddenly a section of life is finished—and we grasp it poetically, metaphorically. A small piece of life, like the end of a trolley line, is suddenly over, closed. Then, abruptly, the curtains open and girls dance out, very energetically: a strong dramatic, ironic moment in itself, and conveyed by strongly theatrical means. The curtain travels right to left and continues off, like a trolley, and the girls go off with it, leaving a bare, foggy stage, and the lone figure of the entertainer, going home. That's exactly it, the kind of effect I love; it uses suggestiveness to wake associations in the viewer. Of course, it's something that must be handled very deliberately, because it could be banal. It reminds me of Beethoven, a genius at introducing, using, then dropping, and again picking up themes—the sense of proportion, relationship: the great secrets.*

This production prompted Svoboda to express again his acute reservations about any merely pictorial record of his work: "There's a danger in seeing my work in photographs. All the elements tie in with each other and depend on the principle of kineticism; a photo can't capture this, even when nothing mechanical is involved. For instance, the curtain in *The Entertainer:* an ordinary stage device, but here it becomes a curtain of life, a poem."*

Two Hamlets

A comparison of Svoboda's two productions of *Hamlet* reveals a creative process employing similar elements—namely, overt kinetics and principles of

Figures 133–138. *The Entertainer,* showing Svoboda's rendering and its actualization in a number of scenes notable for their blending of interior and exterior, domesticity and industrialization, and for their artistic exploitation of banal, everyday objects for their symbolic values: an easy chair, trolley wires, a clock, embroidered walls, sets of curtains.

Figure 139. Hamlet (Prague), ground plan showing the arrangement of panels for twenty-one of the scenes.

reflection—but shaping and apportioning them in significantly different ways, as well as being guided by different interpretations.

The first production, in Prague (November 1959), was relatively austere and straightforward in its depiction of Hamlet as a brooding, scholarly intellectual, intensely engaged in sifting and probing the contradictory experiences forced upon him. The concept on which Svoboda based his scenography was essentially a conventional one: the contrast of the Middle Ages and the Renaissance as expressed visually by the horizontal and vertical, respectively—in this case by a broad flight of stairs and a series of tall mobile panels. The accompanying illustrations and Svoboda's own notes fill in the picture:

Figs. 139–141

> In *Hamlet*, space is formed by the reflection of cones of light that strike the surface of twenty-four panels that measures 10′ x 31′ each and are covered by a special artificial material (so called "plastilak") that has almost one hundred per cent of the reflectability of a black mirror. The lighting instruments are aimed at these black mirrors from the first lighting bridge, so that the actor and details of the *décor* are directly in the reflected light. In this way we managed to get reflected light even into those places where it would otherwise be impossible to aim a cone of light directly; moreover, the reflective panels effectively mirrored the actor and scenic details.
>
> Of course, this light-designed setting would not be of much significance if it weren't supplemented by the movement of the twenty-four panels, arranged in five rows parallel to the proscenium arch, which made for fluid scene changes. With neither a blackout nor the closing of a curtain, twenty-four such

scene changes were effected, in connection with the entrance and exit of actors, the shift of the reflecting panels, and re-aiming of the lighting units.[1]

Figs. 142–144   The production of *Hamlet* in Brussels (January 1965) proved to be an international theatrical achievement of the first magnitude, attracting attention to Czech artistry and craftsmanship as had few events, if any, since the Brussels Fair of 1958. The play was audaciously interpreted by its director, Krejča, and Svoboda's scenography not only caught the essence of the underlying production concept, but positively enhanced it. The set itself, at first glance, suggested a massive wall composed of rectilinear elements, both solids and cavities. But then elements of the "wall" began to move: parts slid forward to form platforms and staircases, while others receded and intermeshed to reveal still further configurations. Most striking of all, however, was the multiplication of this extraordinary effect by the mirror that hung over the full width of the set at an angle of forty-five degrees and provided a reflection of the set as seen from above. One's initial impression might well have been of cubism and constructivism run riot, with the mirror acting as an intensifier of the basic effect. Actually, however, the starting point and essence of the entire scenography was the mirror, and the mirror in turn resulted from the director's special interpretation of the play. Svoboda's reflections on the production indicate the main points of the entire creative process:

> It all started with Krejča and his key to the production: the ghost as Hamlet's alter ego; not Hamlet's father, but a fiction created by Hamlet to gain the support of the people and turn them against the usurper. In effect, then, Hamlet talks to himself, *he* makes the dialogue, and persuades himself. Obviously this is only the crudest sketch of the director's idea, but it suggests what I had to start with.
>
> To symbolize the alter ego concept concretely, a mirror was the only answer, but it had to be a special mirror. I spent weeks torturing myself, devising a whole series of stupidities. Then I realized that Hamlet musn't see himself on the same level, but *above* himself: I had the image of two great birds confronting each other in space. Not a mere reflection, but heightened and amplified. So the basic design solution was a mirror tilted at a special angle. The mirror became the principle of the play; its technical problem was the control of its reflections by lighting; sometimes we wanted a reflection, sometimes we didn't.

1. Svoboda, "Nouveaux Éléments," p. 66. Svoboda's use of mobile screens inevitably recalls Craig's staging of *Hamlet* for the Moscow Art Theatre in 1912. Without attempting to judge the ultimate artistic merits of either total production, it is worth noting that aside from reflecting fundamental differences in interpretation of the play, Svoboda's set was essentially simpler, starker and more austere (less romantic?) in its effect. Moreover, Svoboda's set functioned more successfully on stage because of marked advances in materials and technical facilities. For example, as a recent Craig study points out, "Craig wanted the screens to move before the eyes of the audience, the scene changing in this way without lowering the curtain. This proved impossible and the curtain had to be used after all." Denis Bablet, *Edward Gordon Craig* (New York, 1966), p. 153.

Figure 140. *Hamlet* (Prague). The tall panels provided a sense of classical austerity and dignity appropriate to the low-keyed, introspective, philosophic interpretation of Hamlet in this production.

Figure 141. *Hamlet* (Prague). Photographs of Svoboda's model indicate the importance of the lighting and the special reflecting surfaces of the panels to the production.

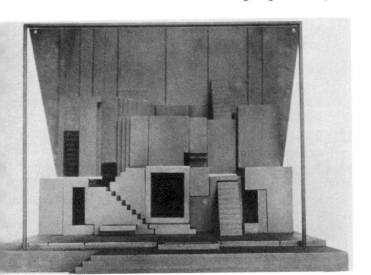

Figure 142. The model for the Brussels *Hamlet* (1965), indicating the placement of the mirror in relation to the central scenic unit, a massive wall of intermeshing elements. The architectonic set became particularly striking with the introduction of movement of the individual scenic units.

Figure 143. *Hamlet*. A photograph of the actual production shows Hamlet confronting his alter-ego in the battlement scene.

Figure 144. *Hamlet* (Brussels). The extended series of photographs of Svoboda's model captures some of startling variations resulting from movable scenery in conjunction with a mirror.

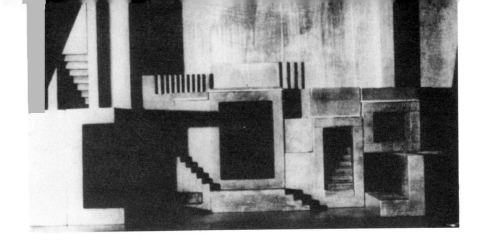

The final step came about as a result of my picking at the model of the set one day after gazing at it for a long time; I wasn't quite satisfied. In any case, I pushed one piece and suddenly saw the reflection of the movement in the mirror. And suddenly I saw Elsinore as a certain spiritual world, a microcosm of Hamlet's world, one which must change psycho-plastically along with the development of the action. It became a world that grinds and weighs on man; it suggested the atmosphere of the Middle Ages, a castle without feeling, anti-human. Obviously we had models enough for this: the Nazi occupation as well as the Stalin era. In other words, Elsinore was represented ultra-flexibly, plastically. The photographs suggest a sheer mass of cubes, solid and fixed, but in performance only selected portions were visible as a result of controlled lighting and movement. The set was extremely *playable*, not as puristic and austere as the photos suggest.

In fact, it became an *instrument* with many possibilities; a good example of the technical becoming an instrument, a means.*[2]

Indeed, it is possible to view the set in at least three ways: symbolically, as suggesting an inhuman, irresistible, crushing mass; functionally, as an embodiment of the alter ego interpretation; and theatrically, as an instrument for performance.

The scenography as a whole bears an obvious kinship to several other productions in its use of kinetics and mirrors, notably that of *Romeo and Juliet* and *The Insect Comedy*. The relation to the former is especially evident in the principle of creating psycho-plastic space by means of three-dimensional kinetics: the movement of solid masses in space. Both productions, moreover, classically embody Svoboda's abstract formulation of movement being the manifestation of the duality of matter and immaterial energy (see pp. 30–31). Nevertheless, the scenography of the productions is markedly different in

2. On another occasion, Svoboda said, "What I tried to create was the organism of Elsinore Castle as an acting machine, not a symbolic one." Svoboda, "Designing for the Stage," *Opera* (August 1967), p. 634.

Figure 145. The Anabaptists, a frontal view of the set. Constructed of solid timbers, it connoted a globe, a city square, battlements, and it made a superb stage for acting.
Figure 146. The Anabaptists. This scene depicts the siege of a city.

tone and specific intention, the scenography of *Romeo and Juliet,* for example, being architecturally more complex and evoking a feeling of lightness and grace that is deliberately avoided in the more monolithic dynamics of the Brussels *Hamlet.* At the same time, of course, one cannot overlook the fact that both productions were directed by Krejča.

The relation of the *Hamlet* and *The Insect Comedy* productions (both produced in the same month, incidentally) is evident in the combined use of mirrors and scenic movement, but a fundamental difference is equally apparent: the mirrors in *The Insect Comedy* relate to the total action and are consistently central to the operation of the scenography, whereas the mirror in *Hamlet* is a periodic, albeit crucial, scenographic element that emphasizes the internal state of one character.

Teatro Mundi

Figs. 145–148

Svoboda's set for Dürrenmatt's *The Anabaptists* (Prague, March 1968) has special interest because it represents a marked exception to one of his most consistent principles, that no set should say all it has to say at the beginning of the performance; instead, it should evolve in response to the course of dramatic action. But in this case Svoboda seemed to have no choice: "I wrestled with the problem, against myself, because the solution seemed to emerge from the play by necessity."* The set was dominated by the ribs of a huge globe, formed of massive timbers, with catwalks strategically placed for parts of the

Figure 147. The Anabaptists. The dropping of the previously suspended curtain effectively changes the scene, focuses attention on the forestage, and suggests an appropriate sense of behind-the-scenes activity between princes of power.

action. The globe was joined to the forestage floor by a short flight of steps and was ironically embellished with a ragged, dirty red curtain and a much smaller, solid-seeming globe suspended from the rafters. All in all, in Svoboda's mind, "a *teatro mundi*, the globe with which everyone plays so casually." * The image established at the beginning of the play is that of a new world, which a group of Anabaptists, like a motley, down-at-the-heels company of strolling actors, enters and, in the course of the action, nearly demolishes with their unenlightened zealotry. Svoboda's remarks suggest other reasons for the significance of the set:

> To my mind it is an example of a splendid concept for a set without complex, much less mechanical, scenography. The image of the globe is deliberate: the world as a great drama. I almost had to cry aloud when the idea hit me—I saw it in my mind's eye exactly as it would be, and indeed it worked out that way. Dürrenmatt, I heard, was annoyed at the idea when he first heard about it, but was very enthusiastic when he saw it here. In our social, cultural context and milieu the set was absolutely right in principle. That's why I like to work here; I know the context, and that makes a big difference. I would no doubt make another design if it were to be done in America. *

It might only be added that the setting, although virtually complete as a statement right from the beginning of the play, acquired numerous variations with the action of lights and curtains, as well as the introduction of various scenic objects both within the globe and on the forestage in front of it.

Figure 148. The Anabaptists, an interesting view of the set from the rear, looking toward the auditorium.

Figure 149. The Tales of Hoffmann (Prague). Svoboda's rendering establishes the chief characteristic of the scenography, a simultaneous scene reinforced by fanciful collage and blatant theatricality.

Figures 150a–c. The Tales of Hoffmann (Prague). Three views of the actual production.

The Principle of Collage

At least brief documentation should be provided for some of Svoboda's freshest, least inhibited, perhaps most extravagant creativity, released after the war and most fully expressed in variations on the principle of surrealistic collage. Time and maturity, as well as the era of socialist realism, tempered the prodigality of invention which characterized this early period; a necessary selectivity and economy helped define and add force to his scenic work. Nevertheless, the following few examples suggest the wealth of creative fantasy at the source of even the most austere of Svoboda's productions. Because the photographic record of those early years is spotty, most of the illustrations must be Svoboda's renderings.

Figs. 149–150   Perhaps the single best example of Svoboda's untrammeled early work is the Prague production of *The Tales of Hoffmann* (August 1946), his first work with Radok and his first big postwar production. Carrying on the tradition of the "liberated stage" of the prewar avant-garde, both Czech and Russian, the production was deliberately unconventional in its use of fantasy, starting with Radok's adaptation of the text, which had the action begin in a theatre costume room and then shift to a fantasy space with several acting levels, including a tiny stage that contained the Venice sequence.

> The key was a liberated imagination, which makes everything possible. The devil, for example, arrives in a mini-auto; fifteen duelists accompany the duel; the white cyclorama shifts to a black one. A large, suspended sphere opens to reveal Antonia, who sits on a chair more than six feet off the floor. Her gown falls to the floor and is drawn by a funeral wagon and a rocking horse; the

Figure 150. *The Tales of Hoffmann* (Prague).

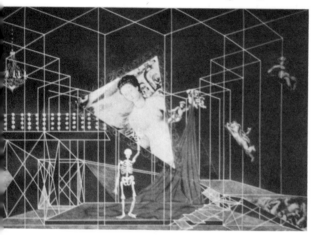

Figure 151. *The Tales of Hoffmann*, Ostrava 1947.
Figure 152. *The Tales of Hoffmann*, Prague 1959 (Laterna Magika).

Figure 153. *The Tales of Hoffmann*, Berlin 1969.
Figure 154. *The Tales of Hoffmann*, Frankfurt 1970.

Figure 155. Wastrels in Paradise, another production characterized by a whimsical juxtaposition of elements. For example, the segmented stars and stripes floating at the top of the picture were previously the pillow and comforter on the bed below.

whole effect is surrealistic. As the opera draws to a close, the gown lifts up and reveals an old theatre curtain that ends the whole opera.°

The significance of this highly fanciful work was perhaps best suggested in a contemporary review:

> The production contains a combination of elements—real, everyday, perhaps even technical—that reveal the deep influence of contemporary technical civilization on our thinking, along with elements that are stylized, traditional, even "cultural." This synthesis of "culture" and "civilization," symbolically illustrated by the juxtaposition of machinery and baroque objects, electrical insulators and flowers, is clearly a new way of representing our contemporary life on the stage.[1]

Figs. 151–154   Svoboda has designed six productions of *The Tales of Hoffmann;* for the sake of comparison, illustrations of four of the others are provided here: Ostrava, Czechoslovakia (1947), for Laterna Magika, Prague (1959), Berlin (1969), and Frankfurt (1970).

Fig. 155   *Wastrels in Paradise,* staged in the studio of the National Theatre in May 1946, was only slightly less free-wheeling in its assemblage of everyday elements and highly theatrical ones to reveal the fantastic relationship of things. Props and other objects had radically different functions according to the action, a projection screen was used, heaven and hell materialized in the midst of snowmen: everything suggested a freedom of childlike fantasy.

1. Jiří Karnet, "Cesta k novému slohu" [The path to a new style]. Newspaper clipping otherwise unidentified.

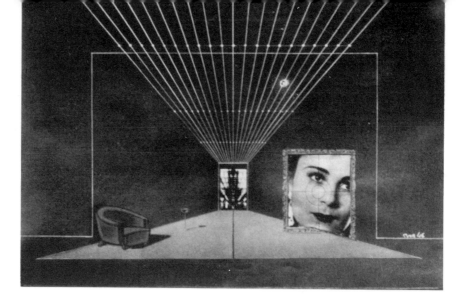

Figure 156. Aibis's Action.

Figure 157. Revizor.

Fig. 156
An expressionistic satire on the super-weapon, *Akce Aibiš* ("Aibiš's Action"), performed in Prague (November 1946), was still another work which confronted a variety of realities of daily life on stage, some by means of film projection, and thus metaphorically suggested new ways of regarding experience. Technically, the production was also interesting for Svoboda's use of forced perspective on an extremely shallow stage.

Fig. 157
A final example of a stage deliberately filled with seemingly unrelated objects was the National Theatre studio production of Gogol's *Revizor* in February 1948, the two basic scenes of which were placed back to back on a turntable. This time, Svoboda jammed the stage to overflowing not for primarily metaphoric reasons, but to capture the sense of disorder, untidiness, indeed rancidness, of Czarist Russia that the play communicates through its characters.

Theatre in Scenography

Although all of Svoboda's scenographic work bears the mark of a sensitized theatrical awareness, a certain number of his productions employ not simply a conscious, overt theatricality, but a metaphoric image of theatre itself. Labels such as theatre-in-theatre, or a stage within a stage, although partially accurate, do not adequately describe the variety of ways in which Svoboda has exploited the traditions and conventions of the theatre to heighten the impact of a given production or reinterpret its significance. For this reason it seems worthwhile to present a sample of Svoboda's notable scenographic variations whose basis or source of inspiration is the theatre itself. Moreover, such works provide valuable indirect testimony about some of his basic premises concerning the theatre.

Figs. 158, 159
The Prague production of Prokofiev's *A Love for Three Oranges* (May 1963) stressed the capricious theatricality of the work by a relatively simple but imaginative shift of traditional theatre placement: the orchestra, which plays so important a role in the action, was boldly removed from its pit and placed center stage, while the acting area included the space above the orchestra pit as well as stairs and platforms encircling the newly situated orchestra. An additional scenographic element was a cyclorama consisting of strung ropes on which projections were cast, a device that Svoboda had employed in the past (*The Story of a Real Man*, 1961, and *Twelfth Night*, 1963) and would employ in the future, perhaps most notably in the London production of *The Three Sisters* (1967) and in *Yvone* (1970).

Figs. 160–161
More complex was the treatment of the Prague production of Janáček's *Věc Makropulos* ("The Makropulos Secret") in October 1965. Part of the ac-

Figures 158 and 159. Svoboda's rendering and a production photograph of *A Love for Three Oranges* reveal the basic scenographic strategy: placing the orchestra stage center and arranging the acting areas around the newly situated orchestra.

tion of the opera, which centers on an operatic soprano, is intended to occur in the backstage area of a theatre; Svoboda extended this inherently theatrical element to the production as a whole. Most of the depth of the stage was designed to represent typical backstage paraphernalia: flats, costume mannequins, ladders, incidental furniture. The action of the opera occurred on a few set pieces in front of this primarily visual background that constantly stressed the theatrical ingredient of the plot and revitalized its point. The key scenographic element was a slanted, transparent wall separating the backstage area from the forestage, where virtually all the action occurred. A variety of projections appeared on and through its surface, and it had the added acoustical virtue of providing an excellent sounding board for the singing.

Two other productions, one early in Svoboda's career, the other quite recent, illustrate a more total, fully organic theatricalization of the basic Figs. 162–165 works. *Rigoletto* (Prague, November 1947) carried the classical theatre-in-theatre device several steps beyond its customary limit. To begin with, both Svoboda and Radok, the director, were bothered by the opera's naïve plot, its bloody melodrama and pathos. In an attempt to counteract this element, they decided to present the work in the style of Verdi's day by placing it in a somewhat parodistic reconstruction of a theatre of that time. Although a strong element of the historical was present, the treatment was theatrical rather than naturalistic. The total set was mostly grey, deliberately intended to suggest

Figure 160. The Makropulos Secret. The backwards-slanting wall could be transparent or opaque, depending upon the lighting and projection. For this scene the text specified a theatre after a performance.

Figure 161. The Makropulos Secret. Because the script calls for an office in this scene (no connection with the theatre), the slanted wall reveals a projection screen (the manuscript) and also functions as a straight reflector (the initials). Note the top letter "E": an illuminated device, lying horizontally, is suspended above the reflecting wall and appears as the upright letter "E" to most of the audience.

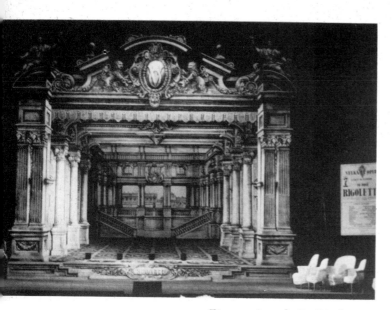

Figures 162 and 163. Rigoletto, two views of the painstakingly reconstructed neo-classic, Bibiena-like stage constructed on a turntable of a large stage; the performance of any work on such a stage becomes at least partially ironic.

a black and white engraving. But the cream of the jest was what occurred beyond these effects, as Svoboda's recollections indicate:

> We made fun of the opera to some extent; the production offended many and caused a scandal, although many loved it, especially those who weren't opera traditionalists. On its own terms, in any case, the production was very accomplished and precise.
>
> I built a tiny Bibiena-like stage on a turntable of the large stage of the Smetana theatre. Everything was in period, including some audience seats in front of the stage. Then, at a certain point in the action, the theatre began to rotate on its turntable and suddenly we were looking at its stage through its wings; the singers proceeded to adjust to this new perspective and sang toward us in the audience of the Smetana theatre through the wings of *their* theatre. Rigoletto, for example, sang his aria to a costumer or ballerina in the wings. At other times we showed waiting performers flirting with backstage gentlemen callers. In other words, the action was presented in the context of the backstage of a theatre. The result was a great charm and a loss of traditional opera-ness.
>
> In many ways it was a difficult production; some singers, for example, had to be replaced because of the exception they took to the production approach. Technically, also, we took pains with all the elements; for instance, the period stage machinery that was revealed to the audience as it looked into the wings was especially manufactured for the production.[*]

Figures 164 and 165. Rigoletto. The rotation of the turntable exposes the normally off-stage part of the facsimile theatre to the audience, and the singer finds himself singing into the wings (and to his fellow performers) in order to project to the modern audience: a provocative inversion and exploitation of theatrical conventions.

A production such as this raises numerous theoretical questions of artistic convention and even terminology. For example, the careful recreation of period stage machinery is in itself close to, if not equivalent to, naturalism; and yet it is part of a larger effort that is utterly anti-naturalistic in terms of the production as a whole. Such paradoxes and contradictions enliven a great deal of Svoboda's work, especially when he joins with a director like Radok.

Perhaps the culmination of Svoboda's use of theatre itself in his designs is the recent *Don Giovanni* in Prague (February 1969), a production that by its very nature must remain unique. Several historical facts are central to the final scenographic solution: Mozart composed *Don Giovanni* in Prague and conducted its premiere, also in Prague, in a theatre that is still in use, essentially with the same interior *décor* as in Mozart's day; today it is known as the Tyl Theatre and forms one of the three units that comprise the National Theatre. Svoboda had designed numerous productions of *Don Giovanni* previously, both in Czechoslovakia and abroad, but this one was to be different:

Figs. 166–168

> My primary goal was to express the unique Prague-ness of the work rather than to employ any certain scenographic approach or get involved with customary scenic details. The design was deliberately non-repeatable, with meaning only in Prague; specifically, I saw the opera in the context of the Tyl Theatre, where it had its original premiere.*

Figure 166. Don Giovanni (Prague). The boxes at the right and left of the photograph are part of the eighteenth-century theatre in Prague in which the production is performed; the rest of the boxes were especially built for the production and are situated on the stage itself, an extension of the historical auditorium.

Svoboda's concept has the richness and immediacy of a Shakespearian metaphor: the Mozartian decor of the Tyl Theatre auditorium is extended onto the stage itself to form the setting of the opera's action. The opera that was written in Prague, to a great extent *for* Prague, and originally performed in Prague, in this very theatre, is now performed not only in the same theatre but within a setting that is a duplicate of the theatre interior in which it was originally performed and is now performed again. The resultant effect, with its multiple reverberations, is dense and powerful and, above all, uplifting in its absolute rightness. It is theatre in theatre, *transcended.*[1]

The customary separation of stage and auditorium vanishes: the boxes nearest the stage are repeated (more precisely, continued) on the stage itself, and the acting area includes the first set of auditorium boxes as well as the stage. The rear of the stage is sometimes filled with period backdrops and sometimes with additional tiers of boxes; when the latter occurs, as it does in the climactic scene of the ball, Svoboda's intention achieves its strongest statement.

1. The nearest theatrical analogue that occurs to me is the use of a model house in the living room of the house represented by the model, in Edward Albee's *Tiny Alice.*

Figure 167. Don Giovanni (Prague): a different arrangement of the on-stage boxes deliberately revealing a period backdrop to heighten the sense of theatricality.

Figure 168. Don Giovanni (Prague), showing still another arrangement of the on-stage boxes, a different backdrop, and a fence that functions both realistically and conventionally in several scenes of the production.

Svoboda's remarks suggest additional implications inherent in his concept:

> The whole design is keyed on the ball in scene seven, the peak of the opera; the use of boxes on stage and in the auditorium makes for all possible variations and has a positive function in the action.
>
> I deliberately used aged, period, somewhat deteriorated theatrical objects, props, even chandeliers, from Mozart's time, and deliberately revealed old painted backdrops and curtains between the boxes on stage or else as total backdrops. I wanted to evoke the feel of an old eighteenth-century theatre—the feeling of the "ghosts" of theatre. A person with imagination really feels the ultimate significance of a curtain; a theatre; a stage; an auditorium; and their relationship—their naïve atmosphere, their simplicity and plainness, yet the worlds that can be created there—the significance and strength of theatre in the evolution of society.
>
> *Giovanni* is so definitive and classical and excellent a work—for example, the recitatives in relation to the passages that *have* to be sung. It's a model opera, pure, a work of genius. It's a jewel to begin with, and that's why I wanted to treat it with the least fuss: a singer comes forward and sings, the others simply stand and wait. The result is an operatic holiday. The spectator doesn't look for naturalism; he accepts it as a pure theatrical work, specifically an opera—a pure experience. It doesn't pretend to be more or other than opera. For example, the grill-work fence functions in several ways, conventionally—it operates according to *theatrical logic*.*

The *Giovanni* scenography may be considered from still another perspective; that is, as one example (admittedly limited) of Svoboda's flexible ideal of *production* space: space that encompasses both stage and auditorium, and that is deliberately created or modified to respond to a specific production concept. Svoboda's ideal would occur in an ultra-flexible atelier; the *Giovanni* variation of the ideal is a result of adapting to a specific theatrical environment.

Svoboda's final observations about this production are worth considering in light of his experience with more than one hundred opera productions:

> This approach to an opera—that is, exploiting its unique historical background, presenting it more à la concert, with emphasis on the singers, the music, and the orchestra, all of which amounts to a different production style—recommends itself for other dated, celebrated operas.*

For most artists, the reputation held by Svoboda during the last few years would mark a culmination and final plateau: honors, awards, a Professor's Chair at the school of architecture where he studied less than twenty years ago, and commissions from the theatre capitals of the world. But for several reasons it seems highly unlikely that Svoboda will rest on these achievements.

His sheer zest and enthusiasm not only for new technical means of expression but also for the play or the game of theatre has not waned since his youth. He is unable to resist the fresh challenge of a new or familiar text, a new problem to be mastered, whether it be a new theatre or a new material, or the satisfaction of working with a special creative partner. For in the broadest sense, like all true artists, he cannot *not* continue creating and striving for ever fuller, more precise expression.

His attitude toward his own creativity was best conveyed in a recent remark, which recommends itself as a final note to this study because of what it reveals of Svoboda both as a man and as an artist:

> I want to enrich the theatre, not save it. Even the simplest innovation can be miraculous.*

APPENDICES AND SELECTED BIBLIOGRAPHY

APPENDIX A

A Selected Group of Svoboda's Production Drawings

Despite Svoboda's emphatic reservations about the value of two-dimensional renderings and sketches of stage settings, I do believe that it is worth presenting a few more of his own drawings as an indication of his fresh response to a variety of scenographic problems. Above all, this brief survey brings into focus his most fundamental concern in scenography: space. His strong architectural background undoubtedly accounts for his masterful employment of structural forms, but it is also likely that it explains his preoccupation with the profounder artistic questions of the division, containment, and shaping of space appropriate to the interpretative and theatrical demands of a given production. Special lighting, projections, mirrors, and kinetic scenery all help to solve problems of production space, but the ultimate answers lie in the classical architectural elements of volume and mass, axis and plane, as the following drawings reveal. The occasional recurrence of a few techniques is perhaps worth noting as an example of Svoboda's "signature": intersecting planes, both straight and curved; asymmetrically arranged masses; one or more frames behind and at oblique angles to the proscenium frame; frequent use of varied levels, ramps, and stairs.

The drawings are arranged chronologically, beginning with Svoboda's first Prague production.

Figure 169. Hölderlin's *Empedokles*, Prague 1943.

Figure 170. Verdi's *Il Trovatore*, Prague 1947.

Figure 171. Verdi's *Don Carlos*, Bratislava 1956.

Figure 172. Hanuš's *Othello*, Prague 1959.

A Selected Group of Svoboda's Production Drawings   149

Figure 173. Dvořák's *Rusalka*, Prague 1960.

Figure 174. Shaw's *Saint Joan*, Pilsen 1961.

Figure 175. Martinů's *Julieta*, Prague 1963.

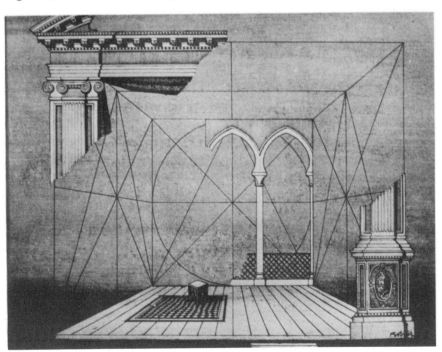

Figure 176. Rossini's *L'Italiana in Algeri*, Rio de Janeiro 1963.

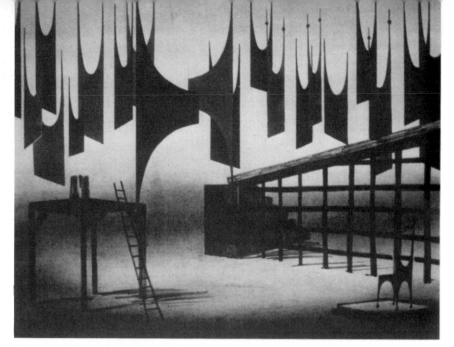

Figure 177. Weinberger's *Švanda the Bagpiper*, Vienna 1963 (not performed).

Figure 178. Hindemith's *Cardillac*, Milan 1964.

Figure 179. Shakespeare's *King Lear*, Budapest 1964.

Figure 180. Bizet's *Carmen*, Bremen 1965.

Figure 181. Gluck's *Orpheus and Eurydice,* West German television 1967.

Figure 182. A rehearsal photograph of *Ariadne auf Naxos* shows the cave platform at stage center, framed by flats with deliberately old fashioned theatrical motifs.

APPENDIX B

Svoboda's Most Recent Productions

During my most recent meeting with Svoboda, in late October 1970, he indicated particular interest in his work on a number of productions occurring in the last half of 1970 and projected toward the first half of 1971. Some of the productions continued his recent experiments, some involved innovations, and others were marked by a bold recourse to the pure, stark elements of architecture, kinetics, stage space, and materials powerful by virtue of their simplicity and metaphoric potential, as if Svoboda were deliberately seeking a renewal of creative energy from fundamental theatrical resources. Several of the productions and production plans are worthy of at least brief description in order to bring our survey of his work up to date and to suggest his latest tendencies.

Fig. 182   The production of Richard Strauss's opera *Ariadne auf Naxos* (Berlin, June 1970), showed Svoboda's penchant for collage to be as fresh as ever, as the accompanying photograph illustrates. The scenography consisted of two contrasting, juxtaposed elements in keeping with the duel of genres inherent in the opera: the romantic and the farcically satiric. A series of laterally moveable panels somewhat reminiscent of those in the Prague *Hamlet* of 1959, except for the "period" graphics on the *Ariadne* panels and their resting on the flat floor of the stage, were in sustained interplay with the other scenic element, a platform with a flat representing the cave at Naxos.

Figs. 183–185   The production of *As You Like It* in Prague (June 1970) essentially continued the sophisticated projection techniques that Svoboda employed so lyrically in the London production of *Pelléas and Mélisande:* a background composed of special translucent screens designed for rear projection and approximately nine irregular, crushed wire-netting pieces that were vertically mobile. These wire screens took front projections but also revealed the rear-projected images that were visible through their netted screen surface. The essential differences lay in the groundplan, which consisted of a series of obliquely oriented platforms in various horizontal planes, in the specially sprayed crushed wire pieces that took projections much better on their grey-violet surface than did the natural wire surface of the pieces in *Pelléas*, and primarily in the special projections that were used on the rear cyclorama screen: fresh, verdant compositions derived from several colored sprayings over various floral, vegetative elements. The final effect was that of a series of delicate airbrushed stencil renderings, very much in keeping with the play's theme of escape to nature.

Figures 183–185. Three views of the setting for *As You Like It* showing various combinations of projections and the placement of crumpled-wire screens.

Figure 186. Waiting for Godot. Svoboda's photographic rendering reveals the kinship of the scenographic principle to that of the Prague *Giovanni:* an extension of the auditorium boxes onto the stage. Of especial interest in the *Godot* production was the large, multi-panelled mirrored surface that formed the rear wall of the stage. Here it reflects the rear loges of the auditorium as well as the stage itself.

Fig. 186   Svoboda's design for a production of Beckett's *Waiting for Godot* (Salzburg, August 1970), provided a variation of the Prague *Giovanni.* Once again, the architecture of a theatre auditorium was extended on to the stage to provide a background for dramatic action, and conscious theatricality, theatre as theatre, was emphasized. Within these general similarities, however, the production (directed by Otomar Krejča) aimed at an effect of more radical shock. Set center stage in glaring contrast to the pseudo-baroque architecture of auditorium and stage was a dying willow tree. The original scenographic concept called for a real tree taken directly from the outdoors, but a shift in Krejča's directorial concept resulted in the artificial piece depicted in the illustration.

Still another new element (in relation to *Giovanni*) was the use of a large mirrored surface that formed the rear wall of the stage and reflected the audience as well as the stage; the effect was that of spectators sitting at both ends of the stage. Moreover, the mirror was covered with scrim, so that when lighted from the side its reflecting properties disappeared; in other words, its reflection of the audience was controllable.

A particularly startling effect was that of the moon, created by the reflection in the background mirror of an illuminated disk actually located in the rear balcony of the auditorium.

Svoboda's return to a relatively austere, yet theatrically powerful scenography is nowhere more evident than in the Prague production of Brecht's

Figs. 187–190 *Mother Courage* (October 1970). Recalling in some respects the kinetics of *Romeo and Juliet* and the employment of a single stark image in *The Anabaptists* (but here a mobile one), the scene created for *Mother Courage* is the result of a search for a concentrated, distilled scenic metaphor—one that would be strong in effect, yet force nothing on the viewer.

In discussing various elements that influenced his work on the production, Svoboda referred to administrative changes in the National Theatre that indicated that *Mother Courage* might be his last production there during his tenure in the combined position of chief designer and technical director: "So I poured all my strength into it, including the technical forces at my disposal." * The guest director, Jan Kačer, a young man who is resident director at one of Prague's innovative chamber theatres, the Činoherní, was a former student of Svoboda's at the Theatre Academy. "We understand each other," Svoboda said, "and worked well together. I had a good feeling of free creativity, as I did with Krejča and Radok." *

Above all, however, was the challenge posed by Brecht, whose work Svoboda had confronted only once before, in a not very satisfactory production of *The Three Penny Opera* in Munich in 1968.

> Brecht hung over me like the sword of Damocles and provoked me. Now I had the opportunity to stage him here at home. I wanted to try my hand at Brecht—even if controversially—to show that it's possible to approach his work differently and yet have authentic Brecht. I searched for an expressive symbol, yet not only a symbol but also something that "plays." I think that I found a successful answer, and a new concept for Brecht production. And in doing so, I

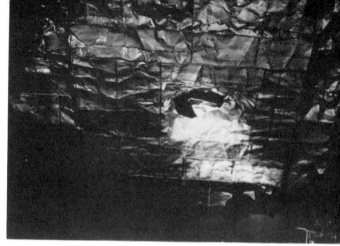

Figure 187. Mother Courage, showing the top surface of the sheet-metal mass tilted toward the audience. The crumpled, torn, corroded surface represented the battle-scarred earth.

Figure 188. The bottom side of the mass revealed: a suggestion of glistening armor, the other side of war's coin.

Figure 189. Suspended and hovering, the sheet-metal object also connotes a certain protectiveness.

Figure 190a. The sheet metal functions as a roof, on which Katrin beats a drum to rouse the populace.

think that I've managed to contribute a word or two to the continuing Brecht discussion.*

Svoboda's answer eliminates such traditionally Brechtian scenic elements as suspended or projected place-names, dates, titles, and editorial comments. Instead, we are confronted with a huge, rusty, irregularly crumpled sheetmetal mass, roughly in the form of a pan, weighing over three tons and having an average diameter of over forty feet. Its top surface is torn, gouged, and corroded, but its undersurface is left shiny, like armor.

> How did I arrive at this precise symbol? I wanted to create the scene from material that would be appropriate to the period and its atmosphere. War, and at the same time, great impoverishment. At times glittering, blazing with war, but actually chewed up, ravaged. An all-out statement. It stands for the earth, scarred with the iron and blood of the war, thirty years of armor and weapons, no longer fertile—but also the brilliant, glittering appeal of war.
>
> It is suspended from three points, and is raised and lowered by special motors. A plastic, kinetic piece that moves silently, effortlessly. The kinetics here do not interfere or distract; they are unobtrusive, even though in plain view. The piece can lie on the ground, be raised or tilted. It establishes different locales and creates different moods. The pathetic, aggrieved earth, yet when it lifts and is suspended it becomes protective: the earth as sole friend, protector. Like a soaring bird or a cloud, it sometimes tilts toward the audience and lets us read into its contours what our own imagination projects. And when the soldiers rattle across it, the effect is absolutely that of *musique concrete*—it becomes a musical instrument.
>
> It became a true theatrical symbol: pure, real, *echt* theatre. A marriage of utility and aesthetics in scenography. I've rarely succeeded as thoroughly in this regard. So far, I think, it's my most beautiful thing—as a whole.*

At the time of the writing of this appendix, December 1970, Svoboda is working on a number of exciting productions to be staged during the next six months. Several represent his sustained devotion to the creation of a special theatrical poetry composed of space, movement, architecture, and other raw materials of the stage brought together in an expressive synthesis. A case in point is his plan for the production of Sophocles' Oedipus triad, to be directed by Svoboda's long-time creative associate, Otomar Krejča, and produced at the latter's Gate Theatre in February 1971.

Figs. 191, 192

The scenography is to be based on a combination of forced reverse perspective and a disintegrating, kinetic, architectural treatment of matter, all of which is designed to thrust the implications of the plays at the audience. A massive wall of eight large cubes nearly fills the proscenium arch at the beginning of the performance. "Then the wall suddenly separates, disintegrates, as the cubes glide backward on rails and on overhead tracks that extend

Figure 190b. Mother Courage's grief over the body of her slain daughter.

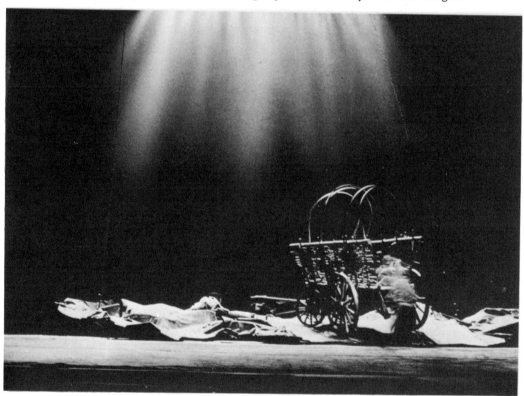

Figure 190c. As the play ends, Mother Courage strains to move her wagon over the broken earth.

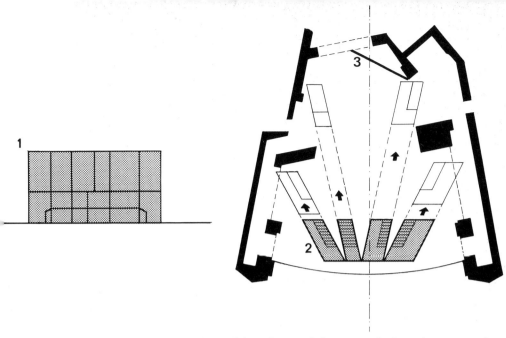

Figure 191. Groundplan and frontal view of the Prague *Oedipus-Antigone* production, showing the reversed perspective employed by Svoboda. 1—frontal view; 2—movable, segmented wooden units with stairs; 3—mirror.

away from the center. We in the audience are the center: the atomization of the cubes proceeds from us. By the same token, the problematic themes of the three plays, perhaps especially that of *Antigone,* are 'aimed' at us, into us: we are the objects of the plays' 'attack.'" *

The scene is entirely mobile, and actors will be able to perform on the pieces, around and behind them. The architectonic basis of the scene reflects Svoboda's philosophical attitude toward architecture as queen of the arts, an equal of music and drama, and superior to painting. "It contains within it all thought and provides a multitude of expressive means. When I first began to use elements of architecture in theatre I wondered, even feared, whether architecture could sustain scenography. It can. It is both art and science." *

A special source of interest in the scenography is the material from which the cubes are constructed: "Ordinary wood, like the old storage crates and platforms that one finds in all theatres, that are the unglamorous requisites of even the most modern, technically sophisticated productions. These essences of the stage, of the theatrical, are here elevated, ennobled: suddenly, as if weightless, they float in the air. We discover the poetry contained within ordinary stage practicables." *

A similar urge to stress the inherent theatricality of stage materials informs Svoboda's plans for the production of Shakespeare's *Henry V* scheduled for Prague's National Theatre in late January 1971. The essentially bare stage represents a universal, transformable space. Defining this space is Svoboda's classically simple scenographic concept: a curved cyclorama of heavy, coarse

193

Figures 192a–e. Oedipus-Antigone: These five photographs from the actual production reveal the variety of dynamic scenic arrangements made possible by Svoboda's concept.

Figure 193. Henry V, showing the relation of the austere cyclorama to the stage floor and the theatrical components in open view beneath it. Flexibly controlled lighting accentuated the black band of space under the cyclorama and the actors in front.

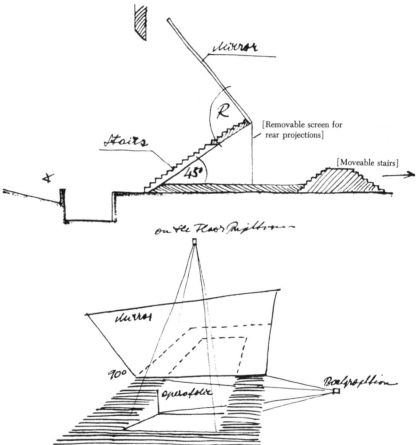

Figure 194. A rehearsal photograph of the production of *Idomeneo,* suggesting the combined effect of architectural elements, projections, and a mirror; and two sketches (side and frontal views) by Svoboda, clarifying the function and the relationship of the various elements used.

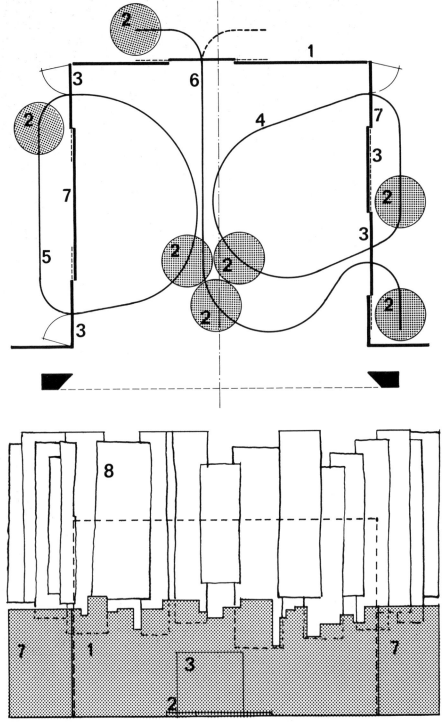

Figure 195a. Groundplan and frontal view of Berg's operatic version of *Wozzek.* 1—Mirrored wall, 60% transparent, composed of segments measuring 150 cm. x 80 cm.; 2—mobile wagons that move at variable speeds along tracks 4, 5, and 6 are rotatable on their own axes at variable speeds; 3—entrances in the mirrored walls that open and close automatically; 7—mirrored walls of 100% reflectibility, composed of segments measuring 150 cm. x 80 cm. All mirrored materials are produced by the Leichtspiegel Company of Solingen and are stretched over steel frames; 8—cyclorama of Studio Folio for rear and front projection, hung irregularly in strips on different planes.

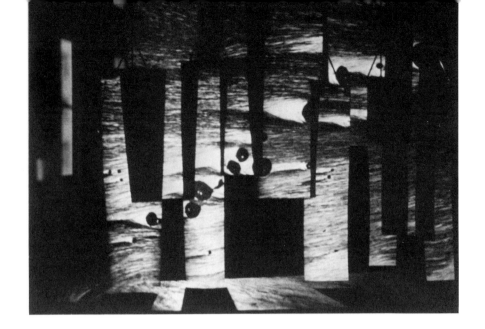

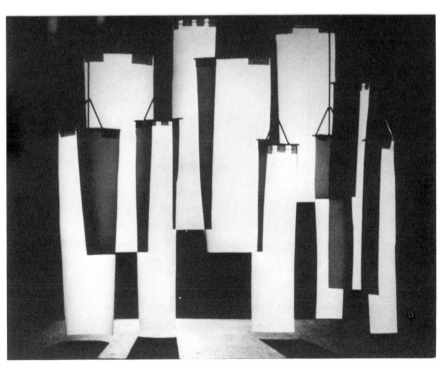

Figure 195b. Two photographs of Svoboda's early experiments with a model to suggest the arrangement and the lighting of the projection strips.

hemp material suspended some seven feet above the floor of the stage and creating an indented black space that encompasses the acting area and allows ready access to it. Within this band of space that rims the stage (beneath and behind the hanging cyclorama) are located the necessary properties, furniture, and costumes that the actors openly distribute and remove during the course of action.

> It creates a marvellous black *relief* effect that thrusts the actors forward vividly. It is a clean, finished space, one that would be ideal for ballet—dancers could enter from any part of the stage. I intend to experiment further with this principle, for example with various projections on the cyclorama. In this production we merely projected an image of burlap to heighten the inherent texture of the material itself.*

Fig. 194

Still another example of the evolution of Svoboda's use of mirrors is evident in his plans for the staging of Mozart's *Idomeneo* in Vienna (March 1971). Taking the Baroque as his guiding motif, Svoboda intends to create a space that captures the effect of a Baroque ceiling. He achieves this effect by having a broad flight of stairs ascend to meet a mirrored surface inclined at an angle of 90°. The reflection of the performers on the stairs creates an image resembling the characteristic Baroque combination of a plastic, sculptured border that blends into a painted scene of antiquity on the ceiling itself.

> The antique acquires a Baroque dimension via the mirror. The basic feature of Baroque interior architecture is the extension of the architecture by painting. The painted ceiling frequently continued the architecture of a chamber by painted elements that extended the whole toward heaven and God. The Baroque thereby acquired a limitless scale, which is achieved in this production with the help of the mirror.*

A remarkable dual project that Svoboda has scheduled for late March 1971 involves productions of both Alban Berg's opera *Wozzek* and Büchner's drama *Wozzek*, in Milan and Turin, respectively, with the same director, V. Puecher. The opera will stress the more universal aspects of the story, and Büchner's variant texts for the play will be used as a point of departure in the drama.

Fig. 195

Svoboda's scenography for Alban Berg's opera will consist of jagged, toothlike mirrored contours around the three sides of the stage to represent the asymmetrical outline of a huge city—a microcosm. Encompassing these mirrored surfaces will be a series of irregularly hung, overlapping strips of grey-black plastic material (Studio Folio) forming an atomized, cubistic surface for projections representing the macrocosm.

> Into this space will glide various objects of furniture and properties on rotating discs, as if in varied orbits, like planets—from the sides and even from the

Figure 196. A rehearsal photograph of Svoboda's basic setting for the dramatic version of *Wozzek.* The raked floor curving up to form a cyclorama wall is reminiscent of Svoboda's production of *A Midsummer Night's Dream.* Also noteworthy are the spareness of the set and the emphatic use of wood.

back—and meet as if fated, then separate again and meet with others or glide off. I want to show that everything that man experiences is predestined, inevitable, and even though circumstances of time and place and society have their influence, basic things can't be altered. I also want to show Wozzek in relation to both the microcosm and the macrocosm, and that's where the mirrors and the projection screens come in. The rear mirror, for example, will be 60% transparent, so that some scenes may be played behind it, or we may perceive some of the objects approaching. Moreover, the mirror will be covered with scrim, so as to take projections as well and thus make the space ultra-flexible. On the strips hanging above and behind the mirrors we'll project a series of visual metaphors: the latest shots of the moon expeditions, the earth as seen from the moon, abstract colored slides, all forming a poetic collage. Wozzek will speak into this macrocosm. I want to show man as related to, dependent upon, the entire universe, subject to certain unalterable laws.°

Svoboda's emphasis on the fated and the inevitable recalls his aim in such productions as the Bremen *Giovanni* and *The Mill,* and the scenic method employed seems clearly related to the unrealized production of *The Fiery Angel,* the director of which would have been the same V. Puecher.

The production of the drama *Wozzek* is intended to bring together all the variants of Büchner's text, not as one consolidated version, but in confrontation with one another — "factographically," as Svoboda puts it — in order to reveal the evolution of this drama. The setting will be austere, consisting of plain unvarnished, unpainted wood that rises from the stage floor to form a vertically curved cyclorama, as the illustration shows. Properties and furniture will be carried onto the stage by the actors. No projections are to be used — only clear, uncolored light of a Brechtian type.

Fig. 196

Svoboda's remarks on his objectives for this production most fittingly summarize his present approach to his art:

> What I want to create here is a theatre that stresses today's rhythms and images, today's manner of apprehending reality. Theatre must be done differently today, but it must remain true to *theatre*. In other words, not a reliance on elaborate, sophisticated electronic facilities in competition with film, but quite the contrary — a return to pure, clean theatre. Not "effects," but thoroughly planned, worked-out patterns based on a distilled, metaphoric concept or image, one that expresses the time, the *moment* of creation as well as of the play — something that I am communicating to the viewer, openly or not, humanistic or whatever — a message that I am sharing.*

* * * * *

In the early summer of 1971, as final proofs for this book were being prepared, I had the opportunity to visit Svoboda in Prague once again as well as to see two of his latest productions: *Noricama*, the Nürnberg exhibit celebrating the city in relation to the five-hundredth anniversary of the birth of Albrecht Dürer; and the Prague production of Prokofiev's ballet *Romeo and Juliet* in the National Theatre. These productions represent the two poles of Svoboda's art and complete this survey of his work through the 1970–1971 season.

Noricama, a ten-minute poetic documentary produced in April of 1971, bears witness to the continuing evolution of Svoboda's infinitely imaginative use of the most complex and technically advanced electronic facilities. The heart of the exhibit lies in a high-ceilinged hall of Nürnberg Castle. The hall is lined with graphics illustrating key monuments of the city, but the focus is that half of the chamber where two sets of panels serve as screens for ten projectors of both color and black-and-white film. One set consists of five rectangular panels of equal dimensions, making a wide wall measuring approximately thirty-six feet by thirteen feet. These panels can be made to glide forwards on rails, separately or all together, a distance of twelve yards, while still retaining their respective projected images. The other set consists of four square panels varying in size from four feet to seven feet and placed well in front of the wall formed by the first set of panels. The usual position of the four smaller panels is horizontal and parallel to the floor and ceiling, but periodically they flip up or down to receive projected images. Each of the nine panels can bear its own distinct image, or one image can be projected on all the panels at once. The resultant collage of multiple images on kinetic projection screens, accompanied by stereophonic sound, does full justice to the challenge posed by the sponsors of the exhibit: to communicate dynamically the socio-cultural history of a medieval city in the most contemporary terms.

Romeo and Juliet (June 1971) is remarkable for the simplicity and theatrical purity of its scenographic concept. Svoboda used his art with complete assurance and masterful economy. The employment of an elevated cyclorama, evident earlier in the Prague production of *Henry V*, was subtly elaborated. In *Romeo and Juliet* the cyclorama became a three-sided arcade suspended some ten feet above the stage by cables invisible to the audience, thereby allowing the dancers completely free access to the full space of the stage. The cyclorama also provided opportunity for more complex composition and movement by virtue of its offering two basic levels with a diagonal flight of stairs joining them. The austere architecture of the arcade, with impressionistic projections, established the locale, the period, and the mood, while the black space beneath the cyclorama emphasized the spotlighted dancers by stark contrast. Svoboda's command of architecture, film projections, and stage dynamics is crucial to this production, but always unobstrusive. His objective was achieved with notable success: the enhancement of the essential quality of ballet—the fusion of music and choreographed movement in space.

APPENDIX C

A Register of Svoboda Productions

The following list of productions designed by Svoboda is complete except for those few done for film and television, certain ephemeral cabaret or revue productions, and those that were essentially minor adaptations of his earlier ones.

I have provided translations of all Czech works when they first appear. Titles of other foreign works are left in the form in which they are generally known in the English-speaking world.

The dates of premieres are frequently difficult to establish with precision; for example, the date of a preview performance is often confused with that of the official premiere. I have been exact in dating when I had recorded evidence; at other times, when I have had to rely on a person's memory, I have indicated only the month or perhaps only the season of the year.

Author and Title	*Place of Performance*	*Opening Date*	*Director*
1943			
F. Hölderlin: *Empedokles*	Smetana Museum, Prague	1 October	J. Kárnet
A. Strindberg: *The Bride*	Smetana Museum, Prague	24 November	I. Weis
K. Běhounek: *Panoš Jan* *(John, the Page)*	Jára Kohout Theatre, Prague	December	C. Sonnevend
1944			
R. Billinger: *The Fox Trap*	Municipal Chamber Theatre, Prague	3 March	J. Kandert
I. Weis: *Kramářské Písně* *(Peddler's Songs)*	Municipal Library, Prague	Spring	I. Weis
J. K. Tyl: *Paní Mariánka, Matka Pluku* *(Mariana, Mother of the Regiment)*	State Conservatory, Prague	not performed	I. Weis

Author and Title	Place of Performance	Opening Date	Director
J. Kárnet: *Bloudění* *(Straying)*	Municipal Theatre, Prague	not performed	F. Salzer

1945

O. Ostrčil: *Kunálovy Oči* (Kunala's Eyes)	Grand Opera 5 May, Prague	25 December	J. Fiedler

1946

V. Nezval: *Manon Lescaut*	Municipal Theatre, Teplice	17 March	T. Šeřínský
G. M. Martens & A. Obey: *Wastrels in Paradise*	National Theatre Studio, Prague	23 May	S. Vyskočil
A. Jirásek: *Jan Roháč*	Municipal Theatre, Teplice	24 August	T. Šeřínský
J. Offenbach: *The Tales of Hoffmann*	Grand Opera 5 May, Prague	29 August	A. Radok
V. Dyk: *Ondřej a Drak* *(André and the* *Dragon)*	Horácké Theatre, Jihlava	11 September	S. Vyskočil
P. Mascagni: *Cavaleria Rusticana* R. Leoncavallo: *I Pagliacci*	State Theatre, Ostrava	22 September	B. Hrdlička
B. Smetana: *Prodaná Nevěsta* *(The Bartered Bride)*	Grand Opera 5 May, Prague	28 September	V. Kašlík
J. Kainar: *Akce Aibiš* *(Aibiš's Action)*	Satire Theatre, Prague	15 November	A. Radok
K. J. Čapek *Ze Života Hmyzu* *(The Insect Comedy)*	National Theatre, Prague	21 November	J. Honzl
G. B. Shaw: *Women's Suffrage*	DISK Theatre, Prague	13 December	I. Weis

Author and Title	Place of Performance	Opening Date	Director
1947			
L. Janáček: *Káta Kabanová*	Grand Opera 5 May, Prague	17 January	V. Kašlík
C. Gounod: *Faust*	Tyl Theatre, Plzeň	15 February	L. Mráz
G. Verdi: *Aida*	Grand Opera 5 May, Prague	18 February	V. Kašlík
M. Maeterlinck: *The Mayor of Stilmond*	Theatre 5 May, Prague	18 February	A. Radok
J. Žák: *Čistka* *(The Purge)*	Satire Theatre, Prague	24 March	A. Radok
A. Radok: *Podivné Příhody Pana Pimpipána* *(The Strange Adventures of Mr. Pimpipan)*	Theatre of Young Pioneers, Prague	25 March	A. Radok
G. Puccini: *Tosca*	Grand Opera 5 May, Prague	4 May	K. Jernek
A. Hába *Matka* *(The Mother)*	Grand Opera 5 May, Prague	23 May	J. Fiedler
G. Verdi: *Il Trovatore*	Grand Opera 5 May, Prague	30 June	J. Fiedler
V. Blažek: *Král Nerad Hovězí* *(The King Hates Beef)*	Satire Theatre, Prague	11 September	O. Lipský
J. K. Tyl: *Čert na Zemi* *(The Devil on Earth)*	Theatre 5 May	25 September	S. Vyskočil
S. Prokofiev: *The Engagement in the Cloister*	Grand Opera 5 May, Prague	8 October	V. Kašlík
J. Offenbach: *The Tales of Hoffmann*	State Theatre, Ostrava	17 October	B. Hrdlička

Author and Title	Place of Performance	Opening Date	Director
G. Verdi: *Rigoletto*	Grand Opera 5 May, Prague	22 November	A. Radok
J. Massenet: *Don Quixote*	Slovak National Theatre, Bratislava	24 November	J. Fiedler
F. Chopin: *Ballet*	Grand Opera 5 May, Prague	not performed	V. Kašlík

1948

Author and Title	Place of Performance	Opening Date	Director
L. Hellman: *The Little Foxes*	National Theatre, Prague	24 January	A. Radok
L. Janáček *Výlety Pana Broučka* (*The Travels of Mr. Broucek*)	Grand Opera 5 May, Prague	6 February	J. Fiedler
N. Gogol: *Revizor*	National Theatre, Prague	18 February	J. Honzl
G. Verdi: *Otello*	State Theatre, Ostrava	29 February	B. Hrdlička
M. deFalla: *El Amor Brujo*	Grand Opera 5 May, Prague	10 March	V. Kašlík
R. Leoncavallo: *I Pagliacci*	Grand Opera 5 May, Prague	14 March	A. Radok
M. Horníček: *Cirkus Naděje* (*The Circus of Hopes*)	Satire Theatre, Prague	19 April	M. Horníček
V. Novák: *Nikotina*	Grand Opera 5 May, Prague	29 May	N. Jirsíková
G. Puccini: *La Boheme*	Slovak National Theatre, Bratislava	16 June	J. Fiedler
V. Kašlík: *Zbojnická Balada* (*The Rogues' Ballad*)	Grand Opera 5 May, Prague	17 June	V. Kašlík
V. Blodek *V Studni* (*In the Well*)	Grand Opera 5 May, Prague	July	J. Fiedler
J. Tobias: *Zlatá Svatba* (*The Golden Wedding*)	New Theatre, Prague	13 August	F. Hanus

Author and Title	Place of Performance	Opening Date	Director
B. Smetana: *Čertová Stěna* *(The Devil's Wall)*	State Theatre, Ostrava	2 October	B. Hrdlička
L. Lahola: *Naši Šli Tudy* *(Ours Went This Way)*	Theatre D 49, Prague	6 October	I. Weis
A. and V. Mrštík: *Maryša*	National Theatre, Prague	19 October	J. Honzl
R. Karel: *Tři Vlasy Děda* *Vševěda* *(The Three Hairs* *of Grandad Know-it-all)*	National Theatre, Prague	28 October	J. Fiedler
L. Leonov: *The Apple Orchard*	Tyl Theatre,[1] Prague	6 November	M. Nedbal
B. Vomáčka: *Vodník* *(The Water Spirit)*	Smetana Theatre,[2] Prague	7 December	V. Kašlík
G. Puccini: *La Boheme*	Zdeněk Nejedlý Theatre, Ústí nad Labem	18 December	R. Jedlička
A. Fredro: *Revenge*		not performed	A. Radok

1949

J. Křička: *České Jesličky* *(The Czech Manger)*	Smetana Theatre, Prague	15 January	V. Kašlík
J. Klíma: *Ohnivá Hranice* *(The Flaming Border)*	Tyl Theatre, Prague	18 January	A. Radok
N. Pogodin: *The Aristocrats*	State Film Theatre, Prague	21 January	B. Stejskal

1. The Tyl Theatre—the oldest extant theatre in Prague—is one of the buildings of the National Theatre.
2. In mid-1948 the Grand Opera 5 May joined the National Theatre; the theatre building of the former changed its name to Smetana Theatre.

Author and Title	Place of Performance	Opening Date	Director
A. Balič –K. Isajev: *Volá Vás Tajmir* *(Tajmir is Calling You)*	Theatre D 49, Prague	28 January	I. Weis
A. Jirásek: *Lucerna* *(The Lantern)*	National Theatre, Prague	18 March	J. Pehr
B. Martinů: *Spaliček*	Smetana Theatre, Prague	2 April	N. Jirsíková
A. Khatchaturian: *Carnival*	Smetana Theatre, Prague	2 April	R. Braun
O. Ostrčil: *Vlasty Skon* *(Vlasta's Death)*	State Theatre, Brno	13 April	J. Fiedler
V. Štech: *Svatba Pod Deštníky* *(The Wedding Under* *the Umbrellas)*	New Satire Theatre, Prague	April	M. Horníček
J. Kapr: *Revoluční Suita* *(Revolutionary Suite)*	Smetana Theatre, Prague	3 May	R. Braun
W. A. Mozart: *Don Giovanni*	State Theatre, Ostrava	8 May	B. Hrdlička
D. C. Faltis: *Chodská Nevěsta* (The Bride of Chod)	Tyl Theatre, Prague	17 May	A. Radok
Z. Fibich: *Hedy*	Smetana Theatre, Prague	10 June	H. Thein
K. Kovařovic: *Na Starém Bělidle* *(On the Old* *Bleaching Ground)*	Smetana Theatre, Prague	16 September	J. Fiedler
W. A. Mozart: *The Abduction From* *the Seraglio*	Smetana Theatre, Prague	12 November	J. Fiedler
A. Sofronov: *Moscow Character*	National Theatre, Prague	17 December	J. Honzl

Author and Title	Place of Performance	Opening Date	Director
1950			
W. A. Mozart: *The Abduction From the Seraglio*	Slovak National Theatre, Bratislava	19 January	J. Fiedler
P. I. Tchaikovsky: *Eugen Onegin*	National Theatre, Prague	3 March	J. Fiedler
W. A. Mozart: *Marriage of Figaro*	State Theatre, Ostrava	31 March	B. Hrdlička
W. A. Mozart: *Don Giovanni*	Smetana Theatre, Prague	26 April	L. Mandaus
A. Dvořák: *Rusalka*	State Theatre, Ostrava	26 May	B. Hrdlička
V. V. Ščerbašev: *The Tobacco Captain*	Theatre Na Fidlovačce, Prague	2 June	M. Janeček
J. Kvapil: *Pohádka Máje (May's Tale)*	National Theatre, Prague	12 June	V. Kašlík
F. F. Šamberk: *Jedenácté Přikázání (The Eleventh Commandment)*	State Film Theatre, Prague	17 June	A. Radok
G. Bizet: *Carmen*	State Theatre, Ostrava	1 July	B. Hrdlička
V. Kašlík: *Lásky Div (The Wonder of Love)*	Regional Theatre, Liberec	22 November	G. Mrnák
G. Verdi: *Don Carlos*	State Theatre, Ostrava	23 November	B. Hrdlička
P. I. Tchaikovsky: *Strevíčky (The Slippers)*	Smetana Theatre, Prague	21 December	H. Thein
Z. Fibich: *Šárka*	State Theatre, Ostrava	22 December	B. Hrdlička

Author and Title	Place of Performance	Opening Date	Director
1951			
M. P. Musorgsky: *Boris Godunov*	Tyl Theatre, Plzeň	10 March	H. Thein
P. I. Tchaikovsky: *Eugen Onegin*	State Theatre, Ostrava	16 March	I. Hylas
S. Moniuszko: *Halka*	Smetana Theatre, Prague	17 March	J. Merunowicz
L. von Beethoven: *Fidelio*	State Theatre Ostrava	28 April	B. Hrdlička
T. D. Čun: *South of the 38th Parallel*	Tyl Theatre, Prague	27 May	F. Salzer
K. Kovařovic: *Psohlavci*	National Theatre, Prague	31 May	V. Kašlík
J. German: *It Happened One Autumn Night*	Theatre of the Czech Army, Prague	13 July	I. Weis
B. Smetana: *Dalibor*	Regional Theatre, Jindřichuv Hradec	July	H. Thein
N. Rimsky-Korsakov: *Coq D'or*	Zdeněk Nejedlý Theatre, Ústí nad Labem	12 September	M. Pilat
B. Smetana: *Dalibor*	State Theatre, Ostrava	25 September	B. Hrdlička
L. von Beethoven: *Fidelio*	Slovak National Theatre, Bratislava	28 September	J. Fiedler
J. K. Tyl: *Strakonický Dudák (The Bagpiper of Strakonice)*	Tyl Theatre, Plzeň	10 November	L. Pistorius
W. A. Mozart: *The Marriage of Figaro*	Regional Theatre, Opava	14 November	V. Kašlík
Moliere: *Georges Dandin*	Tyl Theatre, Prague	19 December	M. Nedbal
Plautus: *The Ghost Comedy*	National Theatre, Prague	not performed	F. Salzer

Author and Title	Place of Performance	Opening Date	Director
W. A. Mozart: *The Magic Flute*	State Theatre, Ostrava	not performed	B. Hrdlička

1952

Author and Title	Place of Performance	Opening Date	Director
C. M. von Weber: *Der Freischütz*	Smetana Theatre Prague	25 January	V. Kašlík
G. Verdi: *The Masked Ball*	State Theatre, Ostrava	25 January	B. Hrdlička
A. Jirásek: *The Lantern*	National Theatre, Prague	12 March	L. Boháč
G. Verdi: *Don Carlos*	Tyl Theatre, Plzeň	15 March	H. Thein
W. Shakespeare: *The Merry Wives of Windsor*	Tyl Theatre, Plzeň	5 April	Z. Hofbauer
B. Smetana: *Braniboři v Čechách (The Brandenburgs in Bohemia)*	National Theatre, Prague	8 May	B. Hrdlička
M. Jariš: *Přísaha (The Pledge)*	Theatre of Czech Army, Prague	17 May	I. Weis
J. K. Tyl: *Tvrdohlavá Žena (The Stubborn Woman)*	Tyl Theatre, Prague	6 June	J. Průcha
B. Smetana: *Tajemství (The Secret)*	National Theatre, Prague	10 October	B. Hrdlička
J. Nestroy: *Lumpaci Vagabundus*	Karlín Theatre, Prague	17 October	A. Radok
A. Dvořák: *Čert a Káča (The Devil and Kate)*	Smetana Theatre, Prague	24 October	H. Thein
S. Prokofiev: *Romeo and Juliet*	Tyl Theatre, Plzeň	21 December	J. Němeček

Author and Title	Place of Performance	Opening Date	Director
1953			
B. Smetana: *The Bartered Bride*	National Theatre, Prague	9 February	L. Boháč
J. K. Tyl: *Kutnohorští Havíři (The Miners of Kutnahora)*	Tyl Theatre, Prague	7 March	J. Průcha
L. Stroupežnický: *Naši Furianti (Our Militants)*	Tyl Theatre, Prague	29 May	Z. Štěpánek
E. Suchoň: *Krútňava (The Whirlpool)*	National Theatre, Prague	5 June	B. Hrdlička
L. Stroupežnický: *Our Militants*	Regional Theatre, Karlový Vary	13 June	B. Stejskal
B. Smetana: *The Bartered Bride*	Slovak Theatre, Bratislava	25 July	V. Kašlík
P. I. Tchaikovsky: *Eugen Onegin*	Smetana Theatre, Prague	2 September	R. Jedlička
J. K. Tyl: *Jan Hus*	Tyl Theatre, Prague	13 November	A. Dvořák
B. Smetana: *Libuše*	National Theatre, Prague	18 November	L. Boháč
J. Drda: *Hrátky s Čertem (Games with the Devil)*	National Theatre, Prague	17 December	F. Salzer
1954			
W. A. Mozart: *The Marriage of Figaro*	Tyl Theatre, Prague	15 January	B. Hrdlička
M. P. Musorgsky: *Boris Godunov*	National Theatre, Prague	12 February	N. Dombrovskij
M. Gorky: *Enemies*	National Theatre, Prague	21 May	V. Dudin
G. Verdi: *Rigoletto*	Smetana Theatre, Prague	26 May	B. Hrdlička

Author and Title	Place of Performance	Opening Date	Director
A. Dvořák: *Šelma Sedlák* *(The Crafty Farmer)*	Smetana Theatre, Prague	1 October	A. Radok
K. Čapek: *Loupežník* *(The Robber)*	Tyl Theatre, Prague	20 October	A. Radok
W. Shakespeare: *The Merchant of Venice*	National Theatre, Prague	8 December	F. Salzer

1955

F. Tetauer: *Zápas Draků* *(The Battle of Dragons)*	Municipal Chamber Theatre, Prague	6 January	B. Vrbský
A. Dvořák: *Rusalka*	National Theatre, Prague	7 January	B. Hrdlička
L. Tolstoy: *The Fruits of* *Enlightenment*	Tyl Theatre, Prague	10 February	J. Průcha
B. Smetana: *The Bartered Bride*	National Theatre, Prague	25 March	V. Kašlík
A. Jing: *The Model King*	Tyl Theatre, Prague	1 April	Z. Štěpánek
M. Stehlík: *Vysoké Letní Nebe* *(A High Summer Sky)*	Tyl Theatre, Prague	23 June	A. Radok
J. K. Tyl: *Paličova Dcera* *(The Incendiary's* *Daughter)*	Theatre of Czech Army, Prague	2 July	J. Strejček
A. Chekhov: *The Three Sisters*	Tyl Theatre, Prague	7 November	Z. Štěpánek
A. Radok: *Stalo se v Dešti* *(It Happened in* *the Rain)*	Municipal Comedy Theatre, Prague	24 November	A. Radok
C. Gounod: *Faust*	National Theatre, Prague	2 December	H. Thein

Author and Title	Place of Performance	Opening Date	Director
H. Zinner: *The Devil's Circle*	Tyl Theatre, Prague	21 December	A. Radok

1956

Author and Title	Place of Performance	Opening Date	Director
W. A. Mozart: *Don Giovanni*	Tyl Theatre, Prague	27 January	L. Mandaus
A. Jirásek: *Otec* *(The Father)*	National Theatre, Prague	24 February	D. Želenský
G. Verdi: *Don Carlos*	Slovak National Theatre, Bratislava	17 March	M. Wasserbauer
V. Nezval: *Dnes Ještě Zapadá Slunce nad Atlantidou* *(Today the Sun Still Sets on Atlantida)*	Tyl Theatre, Prague	23 March	A. Radok
V. Kašlík: *Janošík*	State Opera, Dresden, GDR	April	V. Kašlík
J. K. Tyl: *Jiříkovo Vidění*	Tyl Theatre, Prague	8 June	J. Průcha
M. I. Glinka: *Ruslan and Ludmila*	National Theatre, Prague	29 June	R. Zacharov
A. and V. Mrštík: *Maryša*	National Theatre, Prague	26 October	Z. Štěpánek
P. A. Breal: *Husáři* *(The Hussars)*	Satire Theatre, Prague	11 December	M. Horníček

1957

Author and Title	Place of Performance	Opening Date	Director
W. A. Mozart: *The Magic Flute*	National Theatre, Prague	16 January	B. Hrdlička
P. I. Tchaikovsky: *The Queen of Spades*	Smetana Theatre, Prague	15 February	H. Thein
L. Leonov: *The Golden Carriage*	Tyl Theatre, Prague	1 March	A. Radok

Author and Title	Place of Performance	Opening Date	Director
J. Procházka: *Svítání nad Vodami* *(Dawn Above the* *Waters)*	Theatre of the Czech Army, Prague	15 March	J. Strejček
J. Voskovec and J. Werich: *Helenka je Ráda* *(Helen's Happy)*	ABC Theatre, Prague	13 April	J. Roháč
E. de Fillippo: *The Number One Fear*	Tyl Theatre, Plzeň	1 June	V. Špidla
N. Grieg: *The Defeat*	Tyl Theatre, Prague	14 June	J. Pleskot
L. Hellman: *The Autumn Garden*	Tyl Theatre, Prague	28 June	A. Radok
J. Galsworthy: *The Jungle*	Tyl Theatre, Plzeň	15 September	V. Špidla
W. A. Mozart: *Cosi Fan Tutte*	Tyl Theatre, Prague	4 October	L. Mandaus
V. V. Višněvskij: *An Optimistic Tragedy*	National Theatre, Prague	6 November	G. Tovstonogov
J. Osborne: *The Entertainer*	Tyl Theatre, Prague	20 December	A. Radok
A. Perrini: *The Devil's Never* *Asleep*	ABC Theatre, Prague	20 December	M. Horníček

1958

Author and Title	Place of Performance	Opening Date	Director
A. Dvořák: *Rusalka*	Teatro La Fenice, Venice	31 January	V. Kašlík
O. Ostrčil: *Honsovo Království* *(Jack's Kingdom)*	National Theatre, Prague	14 March	H. Thein
J. Kesselring: *Arsenic and Old Lace*	ABC Theatre, Prague	28 March	J. Roháč
F. Hrubín: *Srpnová Neděle* *(A Sunday in August)*	Tyl Theatre, Prague	25 April	O. Krejča

Author and Title	Place of Performance	Opening Date	Director
E. Radok: *Polyekran*	EXPO 58 Brussels, Belgium	9 May	E. Radok
A. Radok: *Laterna Magika,* I. program	EXPO 58 Brussels, Belgium	9 May	A. Radok
L. Janáček: *Z Mrtvého Domu (From the House of the Dead)*	National Theatre, Prague	10 May	H. Thein
L. Janáček: *Jenufa*	State Theatre, Novosibirsk, USSR	28 June	L. Michajlov
B. Smetana: *The Bartered Bride*	National Theatre, Prague	17 July	V. Kašlík
J. Voskovec and J. Werich: *Tězká Barbora (Big Bertha)*	ABC Theatre, Prague	14 November	J. Nesvadba
J. K. Tyl: *The Bagpiper From Strakonice*	National Theatre, Prague	17 November	O. Krejča
P. Bořkovec: *Paleček*	Smetana Theatre, Prague	17 December	H. Thein

1959

Author and Title	Place of Performance	Opening Date	Director
J. Pauer: *Zuzana Vojířova*	National Theatre, Prague	9 January	V. Kašlík
B. Smetana: *The Bartered Bride*	Smetana Theatre, Prague	24 January	V. Kašlík
J. Hanuš: *Othello*	National Theatre, Prague	6 February	J. Němeček
R. Wagner: *The Flying Dutchman*	Smetana Theatre, Prague	20 February	V. Kašlík
J. Kainar: *Nasredin (The Sage)*	ABC Theatre, Prague	20 February	M. Horníček
F. Hrubín: *A Sunday in August*	State Theatre, Ostrava	1 March	O. Krejča and J. Horan

Author and Title	Place of Performance	Opening Date	Director
G. F. Handel: *Acis and Galatea*	National Theatre, Prague	3 April	H. Thein
J. Heyduk: *Návrat (Homecoming)*	Tyl Theatre, Prague	10 April	A. Radok
A. Dvořák: *Rusalka*	State Theatre, Leningrad, USSR	28 April	O. Linhart
A. Miller: *The Death of a Salesman*	Tyl Theatre, Prague	4 May	J. Pleskot
A. Radok: *Laterna Magika, II. Program*	National Theatre Prague	9 May	A. Radok
V. Kašlík: *Juan*	Tyl Theatre, Prague	22 May	V. Jílek
L. Janáček: *Káťa Kabanová*	National Theatre of Holland, Amsterdam, Holland	16 June	H. Thein
R. Leoncavallo: *I Pagliacci* G. Puccini: *Gianni Schicchi*	State Theatre, Ostrava	19 September	H. Thein
J. Topol: *Jejich Den (Their Day)*	Tyl Theatre, Prague	4 October	O. Krejča
W. Shakespeare: *Hamlet*	National Theatre, Prague	27 November	J. Pleskot
L. Janáček: *Travels of Mr. Broucek*	Smetana Theatre, Prague	17 December	V. Kašlík
F. Dürrenmatt: *The Visit*		not performed	A. Radok

1960

Author and Title	Place of Performance	Opening Date	Director
A. Dvořák: *Rusalka*	National Theatre, Prague	29 January	V. Kašlík
A. Chekhov: *The Sea Gull*	Tyl Theatre, Prague	4 March	O. Krejča
E. Suchoň: *Svätopluk*	National Theatre, Prague	29 April	H. Thein

Author and Title	Place of Performance	Opening Date	Director
E. Illin: *After the Wedding*	Tyl Theatre, Prague	25 May	M. Macháček
J. K. Tyl: *Drahomíra*	National Theatre, Prague	15 June	O. Krejča
L. Janáček: *Jenufa*	National Theatre for Holland Festival, Amsterdam, Holland	July	H. Thein
G. Puccini: *Tosca*	Smetana Theatre, Prague	30 September	K. Jernek
J. Dietl: *Byli Jednou Dva* *(Once There Were Two)*	ABC Theatre, Prague	4 November	J. Roháč
V. V. Ščerbačev: *The Tobacco Captain*	Karlín Theatre, Prague	10 November	H. Thein
V. Novák: *The Lantern*	Smetana Theatre, Prague	21 December	H. Thein

1961

B. Smetana: *Dalibor*	National Theatre, Prague	20 January	V. Kašlík
W. A. Mozart: *The Marriage of Figaro*	National Theatre, Prague	8 February	K. Jernek
B. Smetana: *The Bartered Bride*	Croatian National Theatre, Zagreb, Jugoslavia	February	N. Roje
G. Goldoni: *Le Baruffe* *Chiozzotte*	Tyl Theatre, Prague	25 March	M. Macháček
S. Prokofiev: *The Story of the* *Real Man*	National Theatre, Prague	14 April	G. Ansimov
F. Hrubín: *Křišťálová Noc* *(Starry Night)*	Tyl Theatre, Prague	22 April	O. Krejča
G. B. Shaw: *Saint Joan*	Tyl Theatre, Plzeň	23 April	V. Špidla

Author and Title	Place of Performance	Opening Date	Director
J. Kalaš: *Nepokoření* *(Indomitability)*	Smetana Theatre, Prague	28 April	H. Thein
Z. Knittel: *The French at the Nizza*	Theatre Academy, Prague	April	H. Thein
L. Nono: *Intoleranza 1960*	Teatro La Fenice, Venice, Italy	May	V. Kašlík
J. Patrick: *The Curious Savage*	ABC Theatre, Prague	14 June	R. Hrušínský
E. Suchoň: *The Whirlpool*	Stanislavski Opera Theatre, Moscow, USSR	9 September	L. Michajlov
K. Opitz: *My General*	E. F. Burian Theatre, Prague	1 December	J. Roháč
W. A. Mozart: *The Magic Flute*	Tyl Theatre, Prague	14 December	V. Kašlík

1962

Author and Title	Place of Performance	Opening Date	Director
P. Karvaš: *Antigona a ti Druzí* *(Antigone and the* *Others)*	National Theatre, Prague	23 January	M. Macháček
H. Baierl: *Kurážná Matka* *Flincová* *(Brave Mother Flinca)*	Theatre of Czech Army, Prague	24 February	J. Dudek
V. Šebalin (adaptor): *The Taming of the Shrew*	Smetana Theatre, Prague	30 March	G. Ansimov
M. Kundera: *Majitelé Klíčů* *(The Owners of the Keys)*	Tyl Theatre, Prague	29 April	O. Krejča
G. Rossini: *The Barber of Seville*	Tyl Theatre, Plzeň	16 June	H. Thein
J. Doubrava: *Balada O Lásce* (Ballad of Love)	Smetana Theatre, Prague	21 June	L. Štros

Author and Title	Place of Performance	Opening Date	Director
L. Leonov: *The Apple Orchard*	Tyl Theatre, Prague	30 June	V. Lohniský
B. Smetana: *The Secret*	National Theatre, Prague	8 July	H. Thein
J. Fischer: *Romeo, Julie A Tma (Romeo, Juliet, Darkness)*	State Theatre, Brno	14 September	V. Věžník
J. Fischer: *Romeo, Juliet, Darkness*	National Theatre, Prague	12 October	H. Thein
W. A. Mozart: *Don Giovanni*	Tyl Theatre, Prague	26 October	V. Kašlík
G. C. Humbálek: *Hrdinové v Thébách Nebydlí (No More Heroes in Thebes)*	Theatre on the Balustrade, Prague	16 November	O. Krejča
Z. Fibich: *Bouře (The Tempest)*	Oldřich Stibor Theatre, Olomouc	25 November	H. Thein
I. Krejčí: *Pozdvižení v Efesu (Uproar in Ephesus)*	Smetana Theatre, Prague	25 December	L. Mandaus

1963

Author and Title	Place of Performance	Opening Date	Director
Sophocles: *Oedipus Rex*	Smetana Theatre, Prague	10 January	M. Macháček
W. Shakespeare: *Twelfth Night*	Tyl Theatre, Prague	24 January	J. Pleskot
E. Schulhoff: *Somnambula*	Smetana Theatre, Prague	2 March	J. Němeček
S. Prokofiev: *The Prodigal Son*			
G. Gershwin: *Rhapsody in Blue*			

Author and Title	Place of Performance	Opening Date	Director
K. Opitz: *My General*	Volksbuhne, W. Berlin	4 April	J. Roháč
B. Martinů: *Julietta*	National Theatre, Prague	5 April	V. Kašlík
J. Topol: *Konec Masopustu (Carnival's End)*	Oldřich Stibor Theatre, Olomouc	27 April	O. Krejča and J. Svoboda
A. Miller: *The Death of a Salesman*	National Theatre, Russe, Bulgaria	April	T. Popov
F. Dürrenmatt: *The Physicists*	Municipal Chamber Theatre, Prague	8 May	L. Vymětal
S. Prokofiev: *A Love for Three Oranges*	Smetana Theatre, Prague	31 May	G. Ansimov
W. Shakespeare: *A Midsummer Night's Dream*	National Theatre, Prague	2 June	V. Špidla
A. Dvořák: *Rusalka*	Holland Opera, Amsterdam, Holland	July	V. Kašlík
G. Rossini: *L'Italiana 'In Algeri*	Municipal Theatre, Rio de Janeiro, Brazil	August	G. Ratto
W. Shakespeare: *Romeo and Juliet*	National Theatre, Prague	25 October	O. Krejča
V. Havel: *Zahradní Slavnost (The Garden Party)*	Theatre on the Balustrade, Prague	3 December	O. Krejča
Skala, Fuz, Pantůček: *Drak je Drak (A Dragon's a Dragon)*	Rokoko Theatre, Prague	10 December	J. Pleskot
A. Dvořák: *Dimitrij*	National Theatre, Prague	21 December	H. Thein
A. Berg: *Wozzek*	Municipal Theatre, Rio de Janeiro, Brazil	not performed	S. Ruberti

Author and Title	Place of Performance	Opening Date	Director
J. Weinberger: *Svanda Dudák* (*Svanda the Bagpiper*)	Volksoper, Vienna, Austria	not performed	L. Mandaus

1964

Author and Title	Place of Performance	Opening Date	Director
M. Slomozynski: *Loneliness*	Tyl Theatre, Prague	15 January	M. Macháček
P. Hindemith: *Cardillac*	La Scala, Milan, Italy	31 January	V. Kašlík
G. Verdi: *Don Carlos*	Grand Opera, Warsaw, Poland	12 February	L. Štros
W. Shakespeare: *Romeo and Juliet*	Teatro Mella, Havana, Cuba	April	O. Krejča
W. Shakespeare: *King Lear*	Némzeti Színház, Budapest, Hungary	22 May	E. Marton
V. Kašlík: *Don Juan*	Het National Ballet, Amsterdam, Holland	May	V. Jilek
V. Bellini: *La Sonnambula*	Het National Ballet, Amsterdam, Holland	May	G. Balanchine
I. Stravinsky: *The Firebird*	State Theatre, Wiesbaden, GFR	2 June	Keres and Gora
L. Janáček: *Kářa Kabanová*	National Theatre, Prague	3 June	H. Thein
G. Rossini: *The Barber of Seville*	Smetana Theatre, Prague	3 July	H. Thein
B. Smetana: *Dalibor*	Kings Theatre, Edinburgh, Scotland	17 August	V. Kašlík
V. Rozov: *On the Way*	Deutsches Theatre, E. Berlin	27 September	H. Meves
E. Suchoň: *The Whirlpool*	National Theatre, Prague	13 November	V. Kašlík
J. Topol: *Carnival's End*	Tyl Theatre, Prague	14 November	O. Krejča
A. Dvořák: *Rusalka*	Volksoper, Vienna, Austria	December	V. Kašlík

Author and Title	Place of Performance	Opening Date	Director
1965			
W. Shakespeare: *Hamlet*	National Theatre of Belgium, Brussels, Belgium	13 January	O. Krejča
K. & J. Čapek: *The Insect Comedy*	National Theatre, Prague	16 January	M. Macháček
L. Nono: *Intoleranza*	The Opera Group of Boston, Boston, USA	February	S. Caldwell
J. Offenbach: *Orpheus in the Underworld*	Opera Theatre, Moscow, USSR	February	G. Ansimov
G. Verdi: *Otello*	National Theatre, Prague	5 March	H. Thein
G. Manzoni: *Atomic Death*	Piccolo Scala, Milan, Italy	5 March	V. Puecher
J. Hanuš: *Pochodeň Prométheová* (Prometheus' Torch)	National Theatre, Prague	30 April	H. Thein
I. Turgenev: *A Month in the Country*	Tyl Theatre, Prague	12 May	R. Hrušinský
Z. Mahler: *Mlýn* (The Mill)	Slovak National Theatre, Bratislava	18 May	O. Krejča
J. Suchý and J. Šlitr: *Dobře Placená Procházka* (A Well Paid Stroll)	Semafor Theatre, Prague	15 June	J. Roháč
G. Bizet: *Carmen*	Goetheplatz Theatre Bremen, GFR	4 September	G. Friedrich
L. Janáček: *Věc Makropulos* (*The Makropulos Affair*)	National Theatre, Prague	15 October	V. Kašlík
A. Miller: *After the Fall*	Tyl Theatre, Prague	12 November	V. Vejražka and K. Pech

Author and Title	Place of Performance	Opening Date	Director
J. Topol: *Kočka na Kolejích* (Cat on the Rails)	Theatre Behind the Gate, Prague	23 November	O. Krejča
P. I. Tchaikovsky: *The Queen of Spades*	State Theatre, Wiesbaden, GFR	not performed	V. Kašlík
Sophocles: *Elektra* (Study)	Rome, Italy	not performed	

1966

A. Chekhov: *The Sea Gull*	National Theatre of Belgium, Brussels, Belgium	19 January	O. Krejča
W. A. Mozart: *Don Giovanni*	Goetheplatz Theatre, Bremen, GFR	22 January	G. Friedrich
R. Hochhuth: *The Deputy*	Deutsches Theatre, E. Berlin	5 March	H. Meves
J. Offenbach: *The Tales of Hoffmann*	State Theatre, Wiesbaden, GFR	19 March	V. Kašlík
F. Testi: *The Lower Depths*	Piccolo Scala, Milan, Italy	21 March	V. Kašlík
M. Gorki: *The Last Ones*	Tyl Theatre, Prague	10 September	A. Radok
A. Chekhov: *The Three Sisters*	Theatre Behind the Gate, Prague	1 October	O. Krejča
W. Shakespeare: *Macbeth*	Teatro San Babila, Milan, Italy	6 October	R. Buazzelli
A. Ostrovsky: *The Storm*	National Theatre, London, England	18 October	J. Dexter
T. Wilder: *The Skin of Our Teeth*	Tyl Theatre, Prague	21 October	J. Pleskot
B. Smetana: *The Bartered Bride*	Municipal Theatre, Dortmund, GFR	22 October	E. Vokálek
B. Smetana: *The Bartered Bride*	State Theatre, Mannheim, GFR	11 November	V. Kašlík
J. Giraudoux: *The Madwoman of Chaillot*	Tyl Theatre, Prague	25 November	R. Hrušinský

Author and Title	Place of Performance	Opening Date	Director
B. Martinů: *Hry O Mariích* *(The Mary Plays)*	State Theatre, Wiesbaden, GFR	18 December	V. Kašlík
G. Verdi: *Il Trovatore*	Komische Opera, E. Berlin	December	G. Friedrich
C. Gounod: *Faust*	Teatr Wielki, Warsaw, Poland		L. Štros
G. Büchner: *Danton's Death*	National Theatre, London, England	not performed	L. Olivier

1967

Author and Title	Place of Performance	Opening Date	Director
F. Garcia-Lorca: *The House of Bernarda Alba*	Tyl Theatre, Prague	1 March	A. Radok
Dr. Novotný: *Proměny* *(Metamorphoses)*	Expo 67, Montreal, Canada	27 April	J. Svoboda
E. Radok: *Diapolyekran—The Creation of the World*	Expo 67, Montreal, Canada	27 April	E. Radok
J. Svoboda: *Polyvision*	Expo 67, Montreal, Canada	27 April	J. Svoboda
J. Svoboda: *Symfonie*	Expo 67, Montreal, Canada	27 April	J. Svoboda
R. Strauss: *Die Frau Ohne Schatten*	Royal Opera House, London, England	14 June	R. Hartmann
A. Chekhov: *The Three Sisters*	National Theatre, London, England	4 July	L. Olivier
J. Nestroy: *One-Ended Rope*	Theatre Behind the Gate, Prague	26 November	O. Krejča
R. Wagner: *Tristan und Isolde*	State Theatre, Wiesbaden, GFR	30 December	C. Drese
R. Graves: *The Iliad*	Lincoln Center, New York, USA	not performed	S. Wanamaker

1968

W. Gombrowicz: *The Wedding*	Schiller Theatre, W. Berlin	9 January	E. Schröder
C. Gounod: *Faust*	State Theatre, Wiesbaden, GFR	17 February	V. Kašlík
F. Dürrenmatt: *The Anabaptists*	National Theatre, Prague	3 March	M. Macháček
Sophocles: *Antigone*	Finnish National Theatre, Helsinki, Finland	6 March	A. Kirimaa
J. Topol: *Carnival's End*	Academic Theatre, Vienna, Austria	27 April	O. Krejča
G. Meyerbeer: *Robert Le Diable*	Teatro Communale, Florence, Italy	7 May	M. Wallmann
B. Brecht: *The Three Penny Opera*	Chamber Theatre, Munich, GFR	12 May	J. Grossman
C. M. von Weber: *Oberon*	State Opera, Munich, GFR	15 May	R. Hartmann
J. K. Tyl: *The Bagpiper from Strakonice*	National Theatre, Prague	16 May	J. Pleskot
K. Orff: *Prometheus*	State Opera, Munich, GFR	August	A. Everding
M. Macourek: *Hra Na Zuzanku* (The Suzanna Play)	Municipal Theatre, Frankfurt/Main, GFR	5 November	J. Pleskot
A. Schnitzler: *The Green Cockatoo*	Theatre Behind the Gate, Prague	14 December	O. Krejča
J. Topol: *Hodina Lásky* (Hour of Love)			
R. Strauss: *Salome*	Civic Opera House, Chicago, USA	not performed	V. Puecher

1969

J. Offenbach: *The Tales of Hoffmann*	Deutsche Oper, W. Berlin	1 January	V. Kašlík

Author and Title	Place of Performance	Opening Date	Director
W. A. Mozart: *Don Giovanni*	Tyl Theatre, Prague	7 February	V. Kašlík
G. Verdi: *Macbeth*	Municipal Theatre, Köln, GFR	8 February	H. Neugebauer
L. J. Werle: *The Journey*	State Opera, Hamburg, GFR	2 March	L. Runsten
B. A. Zimmerman: *The Soldiers*	State Opera, Munich, GFR	23 March	V. Kašlík
G. Verdi: *Sicilian Vespers*	State Opera, Hamburg, GFR	4 May	J. Dexter
S. Prokofiev: *The Fiery Angel*	Municipal Theatre, Frankfurt/Main, GFR	10 May	V. Kašlík
W. Shakespeare: *Romeo and Juliet*	Municipal Theatre, Köln, GFR	10 May	O. Krejča
L. Janáček: *Jenufa*	National Theatre, Prague	30 May	H. Thein
W. Shakespeare: *Macbeth*	Tyl Theatre, Prague	4 June	J. Pleskot
R. Wagner: *The Flying Dutchman*	Festival Theatre, Bayreuth, GFR	25 July	A. Everding
A. Chekhov: *The Sea Gull*	Municipal Theatre, Stockholm	September	O. Krejča
A. de Musset: *Lorenzaccio*	Theatre Behind the Gate, Prague	7 October	O. Krejča
F. Garcia-Lorca: *The House of Bernarda Alba*	Theatre Royal du Parc, Brussels	12 November	A. Radok
C. Debussy: *Pelléas and Mélisande*	Royal Opera House, London	1 December	V. Kašlík
R. Wagner: *Tannhäuser*	State Opera, Hamburg, GFR	7 December	H. Mayen
W. Shakespeare: *Antony and Cleopatra*	Schiller Theatre, W. Berlin	not performed	F. Kortner

Author and Title	Place of Performance	Opening Date	Director
1970			
J. Zeyer and J. Suk: *Radúz and Mahulena*	National Theatre, Prague	9 January	K. Zachar
S. Szokolay: *Hamlet*	Municipal Theatre, Köln, GFR	28 January	H. Neugebauer
L. J. Werle: *The Journey*	Royal Opera, Stockholm	January	L. Runsten
H. Böll: *The Clown*	Municipal Theatre, Dusseldorf, GFR	January	A. Radok
A. Chekhov: *Ivanov*	Theatre Behind the Gate, Prague	13 February	O. Krejča
C. Fry: *The Lady's Not for Burning*	Tyl Theatre, Prague	14 February	M. Macháček
W. Gombrowicz: *Yvone*	Schiller Theatre, W. Berlin	26 February	E. Schröder
A. Dvořák: *Rusalka*	Theatre am Gärtnerplatz, Munich, GFR	26 February	V. Kašlík
G. Verdi: *Aida*	Municipal Theatre, Köln, GFR	20 March	W. Blum
R. Karel: *Smrt Kmotřička* (Death, The Godmother)	National Theatre, Prague	29 April	V. Kašlík
A. Chekhov: *The Three Sisters*	National Theatre, Brussels	April	O. Krejča
J. Offenbach: *The Tales of Hoffman*	Municipal Theatre, Frankfurt/Main, GFR	25 May	V. Kašlík
R. Strauss: *Ariadne auf Naxos*	Deutsche Oper, W. Berlin	7 June	G. R. Selner
W. Shakespeare: *As You Like It*	Tyl Theatre, Prague	19 June	J. Pleskot
W. A. Mozart: *The Magic Flute*	State Opera, Munich, GFR	14 July	G. Rennert
F. Dostoyevsky: *The Idiot*	National Theatre, London	15 July	A. Quayle

Author and Title	Place of Performance	Opening Date	Director
S. Beckett: *Waiting for Godot*	State Theatre, Salzburg	21 August	O. Krejča
J. Nestroy: *One-Ended Rope*	Municipal Theatre, Dusseldorf, GFR	6 September	O. Krejča
B. Brecht: *Mother Courage*	Tyl Theatre, Prague	16 October	J. Kačer
G. Verdi: *Don Carlos*	Municipal Theatre, Frankfurt/Main, GFR	18 December	V. Kašlík
S. Prokofiev: *The Fiery Angel*	La Scala, Milan	not performed	V. Puecher

1971

Author and Title	Place of Performance	Opening Date	Director
W. Shakespeare: *Henry V*	Tyl Theatre, Prague	29 January	M. Macháček
Sophocles: *Oedipus, Oedipus at Colonus, Antigone*	Theatre Behind the Gate, Prague	3 February	O. Krejča
W. A. Mozart: *Idomeneo*	State Opera, Vienna	15 March	V. Kašlík
R. Wagner: *Die Meistersinger*	National Theatre, Prague	not performed	H. Thein
G. Büchner: *Wozzek*	Teatro Stabile, Torino	March	V. Puecher and K. Jernek
A. Berg: *Wozzek*	La Scala, Milan	27 March	V. Puecher
J. Svoboda: *Noricama*	Nürnberg Castle, Nürnberg	2 April	L. Rychman
P. Dessau: *Lancelot*	State Opera, Munich, GFR	23 April	V. Kašlík
R. Wagner: *Die Meistersinger*	Municipal Theatre, Nurnberg, GFR	not performed	A. Everding
S. Prokofiev: *Romeo and Juliet*	National Theatre, Prague	19 June	P. Weigl

SELECTED BIBLIOGRAPHY

SELECTED BIBLIOGRAPHY

Bablet, Denis. *Josef Svoboda*. Prague: Theatre Institute, 1966.

———. "Josef Svoboda au TEP." *Les Lettres Françaises* (18–25 April 1968), 1230:20–21.

———. "Josef Svoboda: Scénographe d'Aujourd'hui." *Mensuel du Théâtre de L'Est Parisien Maison de la Culture* (April 1968), 45:1–3.

———. *La Scena e l'immagine*, transl. Clara Lusignoli. Turin: Einaudi, 1970.

———. "Théâtres et Techniques: Technique, espace et lumière, les trois atouts de Josef Svoboda." *Theatre* (15 January 1964), pp. 8–10.

———. "Une Exposition Josef Svoboda." *Lettres Françaises* (5 May 1966), p. 22.

Bartušek, Antonín. "Nové obsory scenografie" [Scenography's new horizons]. *Acta Scaenographica* (November-December 1961), pp. 67–69.

———. "Od experimentu k synteze" [From experiment to synthesis]. *Vytvarní Umění* (September 1964), 14.6–7:251–266.

Bretyšová, Tána. "Tajemství prostoru, světla, a pohybu, aneb Česká scenografie jako pojem" [The secret of space, light, and movement, or the concept of Czech scenography]. *Reporter* (24 April 1967), pp. 31–34.

Bryden, Ronald. "Svoboda." *Observer* (2 July 1967), pp. 4–6.

Burian, Jarka M. "Joseph Svoboda: Theatre Artist in an Age of Science." *Educational Theatre Journal* (May 1970), pp. 123–145.

Casson, Hugh. "Conversation with Svoboda." *Journal of the Royal Institute of British Architects* (March 1967), 74.5:202–203.

"Das traumtheater des Josef Svoboda." *Theater Heute* (January 1969), 10.1:27–34.

DeWetter, Jaroslav. "Před Objektivem" [In front of the lens]. *Divadlo* (1962), 3:24–29.

Groszer, Helmuth. "Arbeiten mit Josef Svoboda." *Bühnentechnische Rundschau* (April 1968), 2:18–23.

Hrbas, Jiří, ed. *Laterna Magika*. Prague: Filmový Ústav, 1968.

Jindra, Vladimír. "Atakovaná scéna" [The scene attacked]. *Divadlo* (October 1966), pp. 43–48.

———. "Dialog II." *Divadelní Noviny* (18 June 1969), 12.20:5.

———. "Dialog III." *Divadelní Noviny* (2 July 1969), 12.21–22:12.

———. "Dílčí bilance" [A survey of works]. *Divadelní Noviny* (29 January 1969), 12.10:6.

———. "Inscenační prostor" [Production space]. *Divadlo* (April 1969), pp. 51–56.

———. ed. *Le Théâtre en Tchecoslovaquie: Scénographie*. Prague: Institut du Théâtre, 1962.

———. ed. *Milan Kundera: Majitelé Klíčů*. Prague: Divadelní Ustav, 1963.

———. *Who Is Josef Svoboda?* Prague: Orbis, 1968.

"A Josef Svoboda Portfolio." *Theatre Design and Technology* (December 1966), 7:23–25.

Kouřil, Miroslav. "Das Lichttheater und die Laterna Magika." *Bühnentechnische Rundschau* (December 1965), 6:9–15.

———. "Uprostřed hledání nové scenografie" [In the middle of a search for new scenography]. Introduction to *Josef Svoboda* [a catalogue of Svoboda exhibition in Prague]. Prague: Narodní Divadlo, 1961, pages unnumbered.

Krejča, Otomar. Untitled speech delivered at Prague Quadriennale Symposium, October 1967, printed in *Zprávy Divadelního Ustavu* (1967), 8:14–27.

"Laterna Magika." *Czechoslovak Life* (March 1959), pp. 13–17.

Němcová, Jeanne. "Josef Svoboda Lights the Stage." *Czechoslovak Life* (July 1962), pp. 21–24.

Robertshaw, Ursula. "Czech Designer Transforms Covent Garden." *Illustrated London News* (June 17, 1967), p. 34.

"Rozmlouváme s arch. Josefem Svobodou" [A conversation with architect Josef Svoboda]. *Acta Scaenographica* (March 1964), 4.8:152–158.

Secci, Lia. "Incontro con Joseph Svoboda." *Sipario* (April 1965), 228:6–8.

Solncevá, L. P. "Der Regisseur und der Bühnenbildner." *Interscena* (Winter 1967), 5:28–53.

Strzelecki, Zenobiusz. "Josef Svoboda's Theatre." *Projekt*, 5 67/1968, p. 28.

Svoboda, Josef. "Designing for the Stage." *Opera* (August 1967), 18.8:631–636.

———. "Možnosti a potřeby" [Possibilities and needs]. *Divadlo* (September 1967), pp. 7–11.

———. "O světelném divadle" [On the theatre of light]. *Informační Zprávy Scenografické Laboratoře* (September 1958), pp. 4–6.

———. "Přestárlý problem" [An ancient problem]. *Divadlo* (February 1968), pp. 44–46.

———. "Rozhovory se scenografy" [Conversations with scenographers]. *Acta Scaenographica* (January 1969), 9.6:104–106.

———. "Scéna přítomnosti a budoucnosti" [The setting today and tomorrow]. *Ochotnické Divadlo* (1959), 5.5:108–109.

———. "Scéna v diskusi" [Discussion about scenery]. *Divadlo* (May 1966), pp. 2–3.

———. "Svobodovský monolog" [A Svoboda monologue]. *Divadlo* (1964), 1:72–76.

———. "Szenographie als Teil der Aufführung." *Bühnentechnische Rundschau* (December 1968), 6:11–13.

———. Untitled speeches delivered at Prague Quadriennale Symposium, October 1967, printed in *Zprávy Divadelního Ústavu* (1967), 8:27–34, 45–48.

Waterhouse, Robert. "The Designer Talks." *Plays and Players* (August 1970), pp. 24, 58.